4th of July Coloring Book: A Patriotic Activity Book to Celebrate Being Too Cool for British Rule in America

Hi everyone,

Thank you so much for purchasing this coloring book. I hope you enjoy it!

I have a special surprise for you…

Claim your gift here: https://bit.ly/2K58AtH

Thanks so much and happy coloring!

© 2018 Annie Clemens

All Rights Reserved.

This book or parts thereof may not be reproduced in any form, stored in any retrieval system, or transmitted in any form by any means—electronic, mechanical, photocopy, recording, or otherwise—without prior written permission of the Publisher

Color Test Page

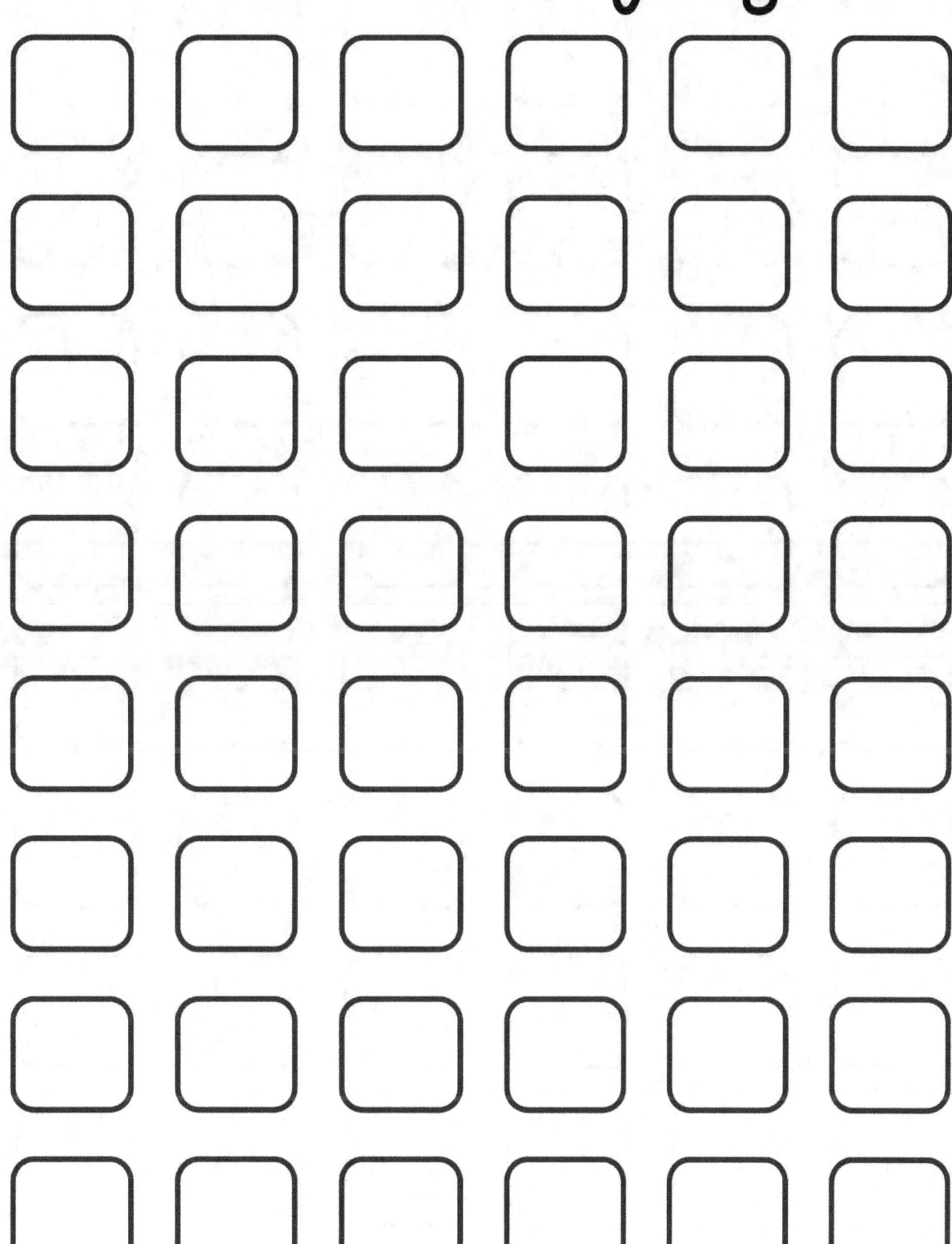

Color Test Page

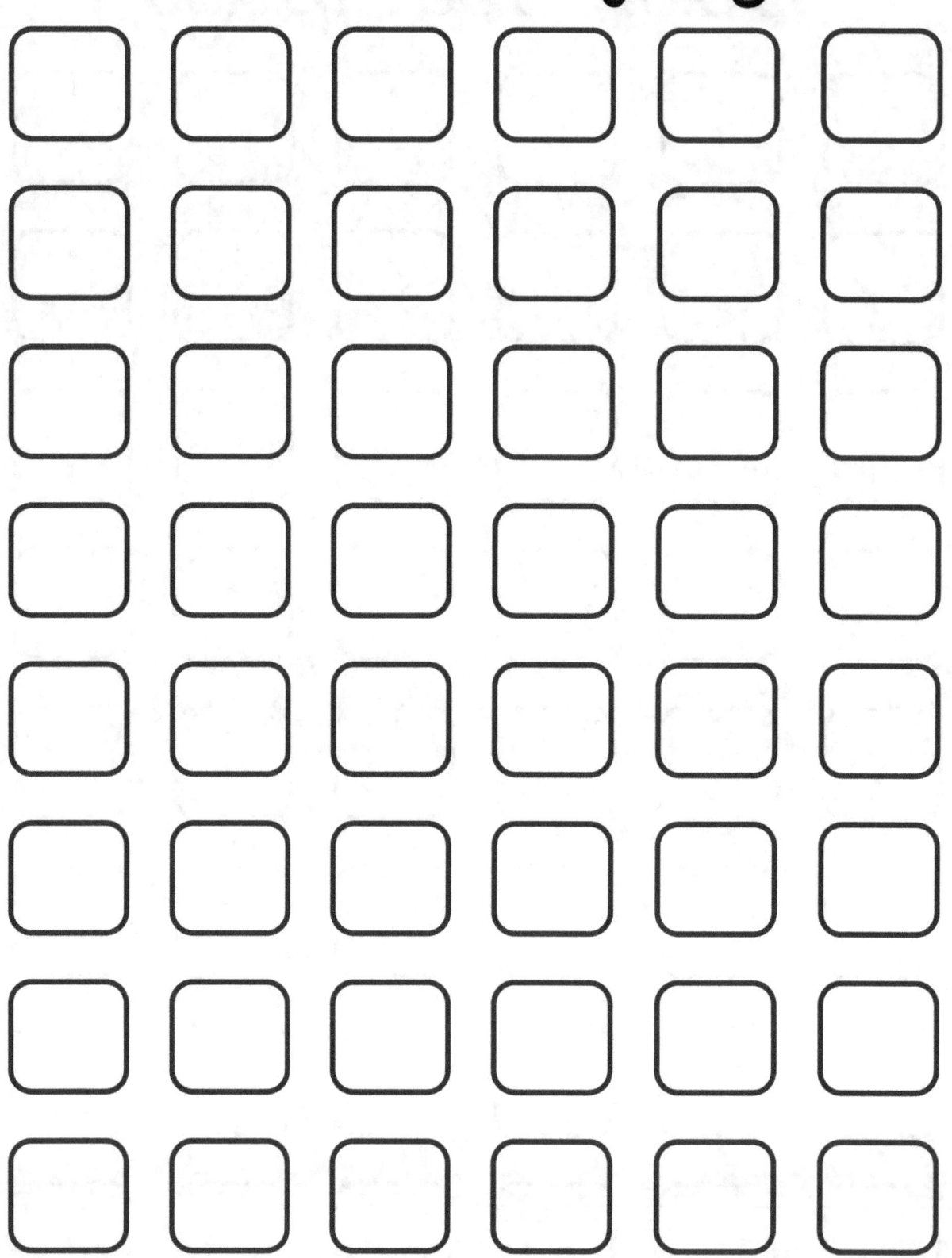

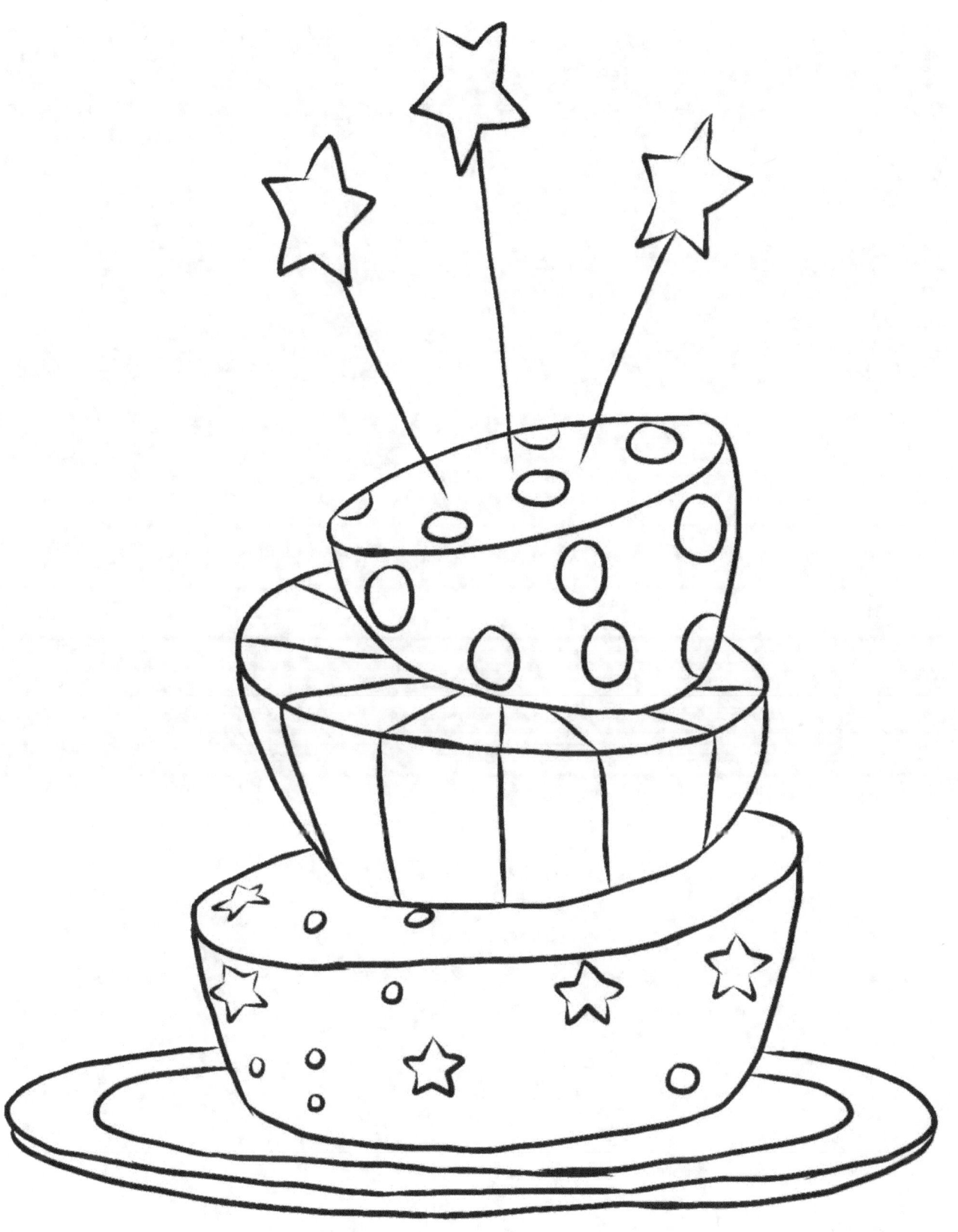

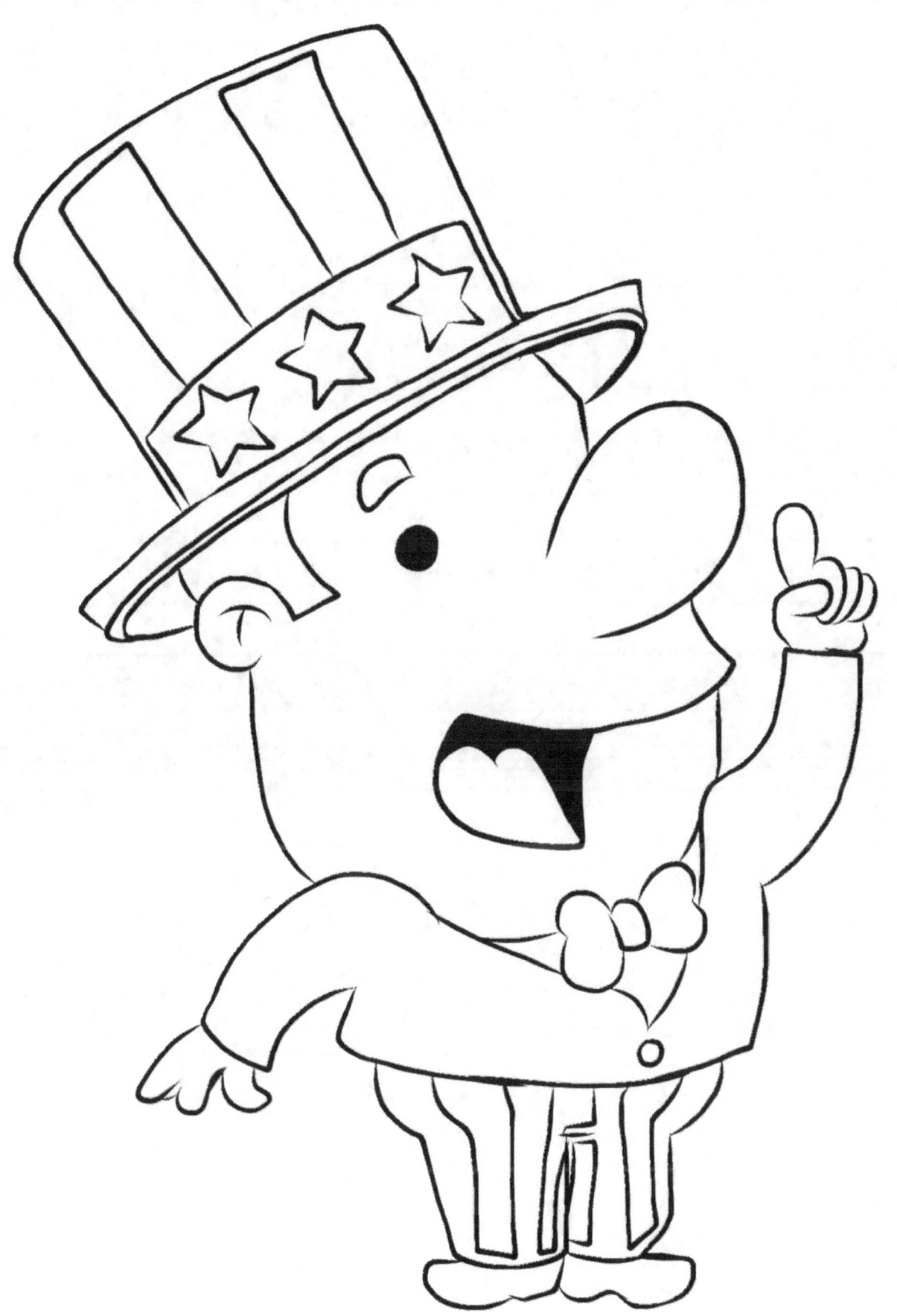

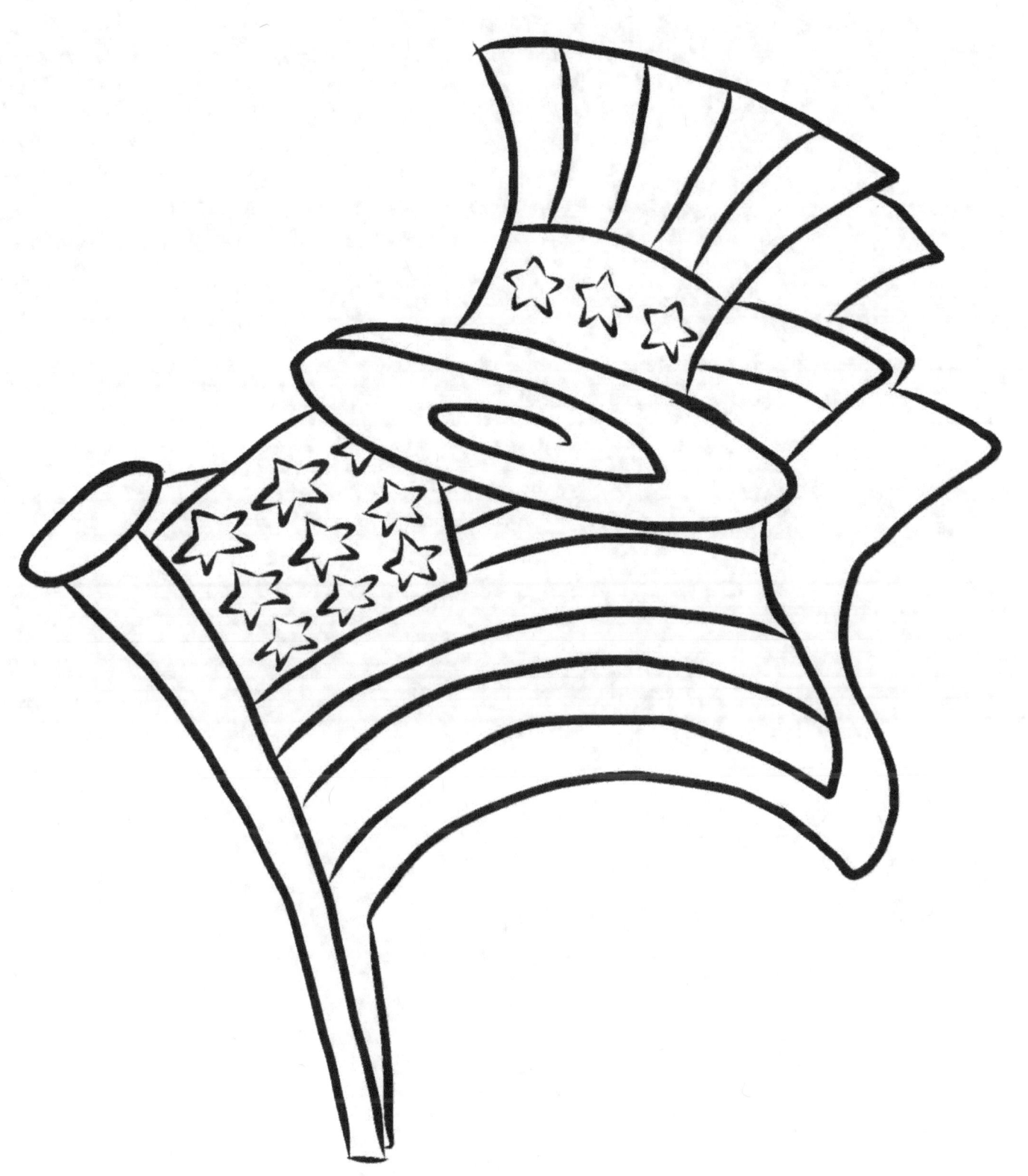

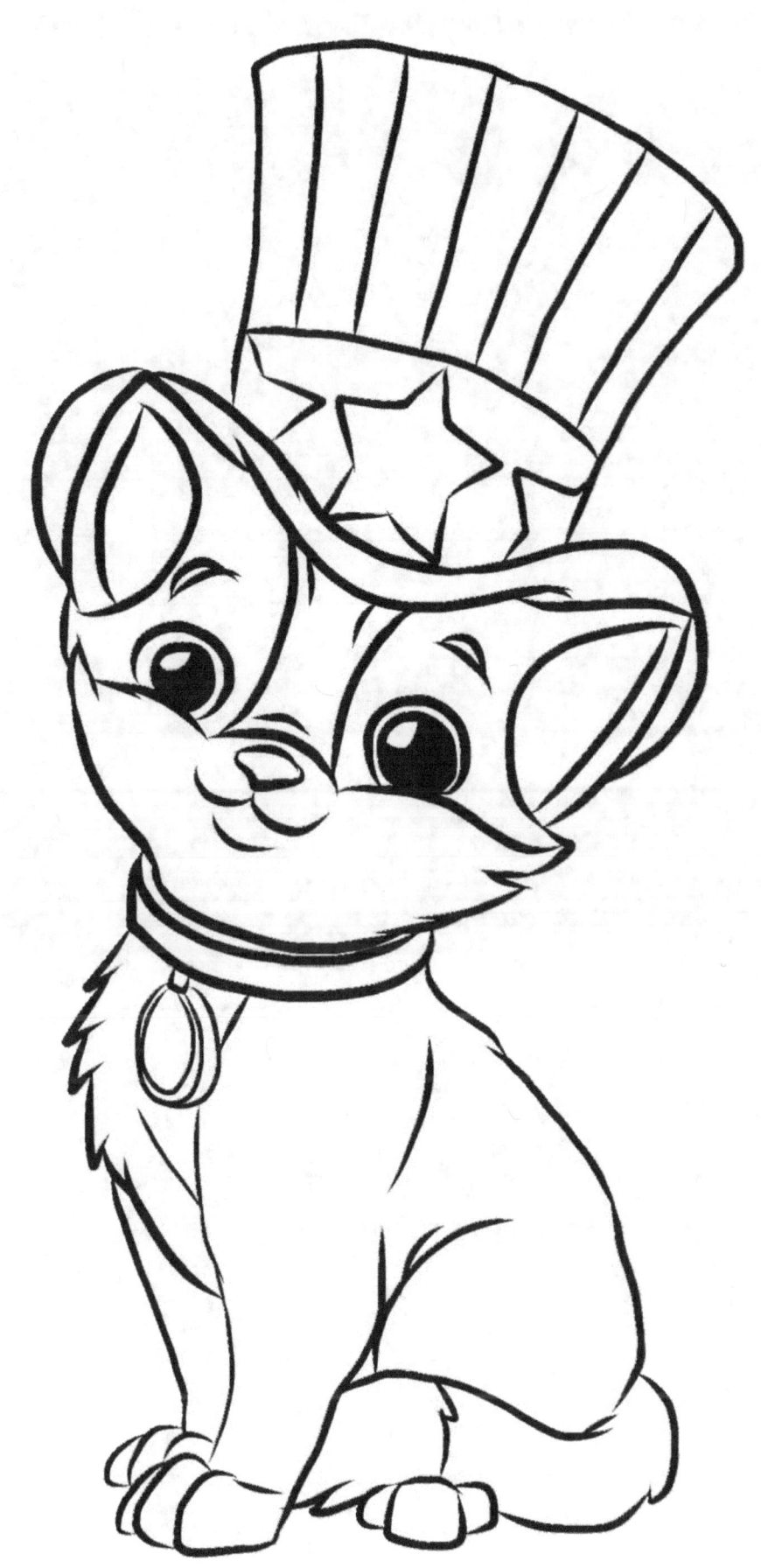

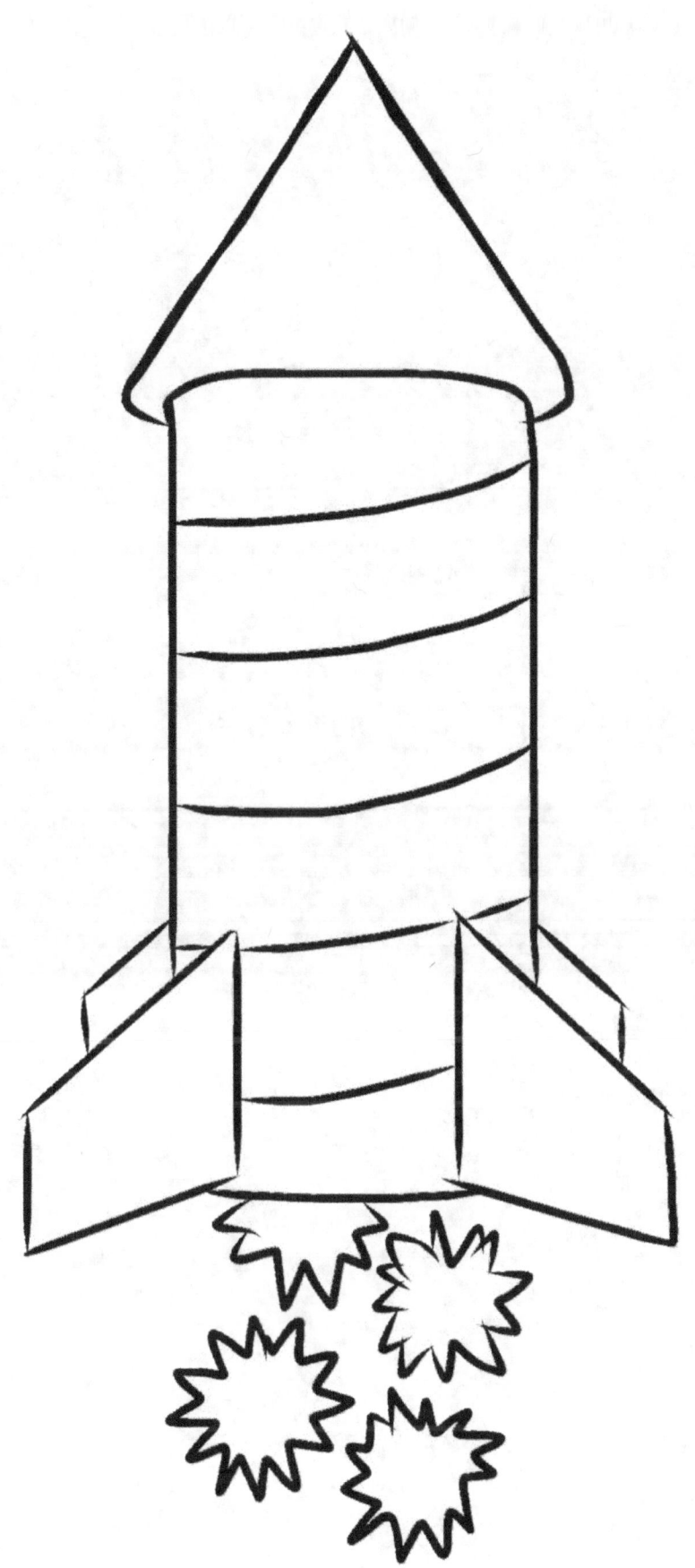

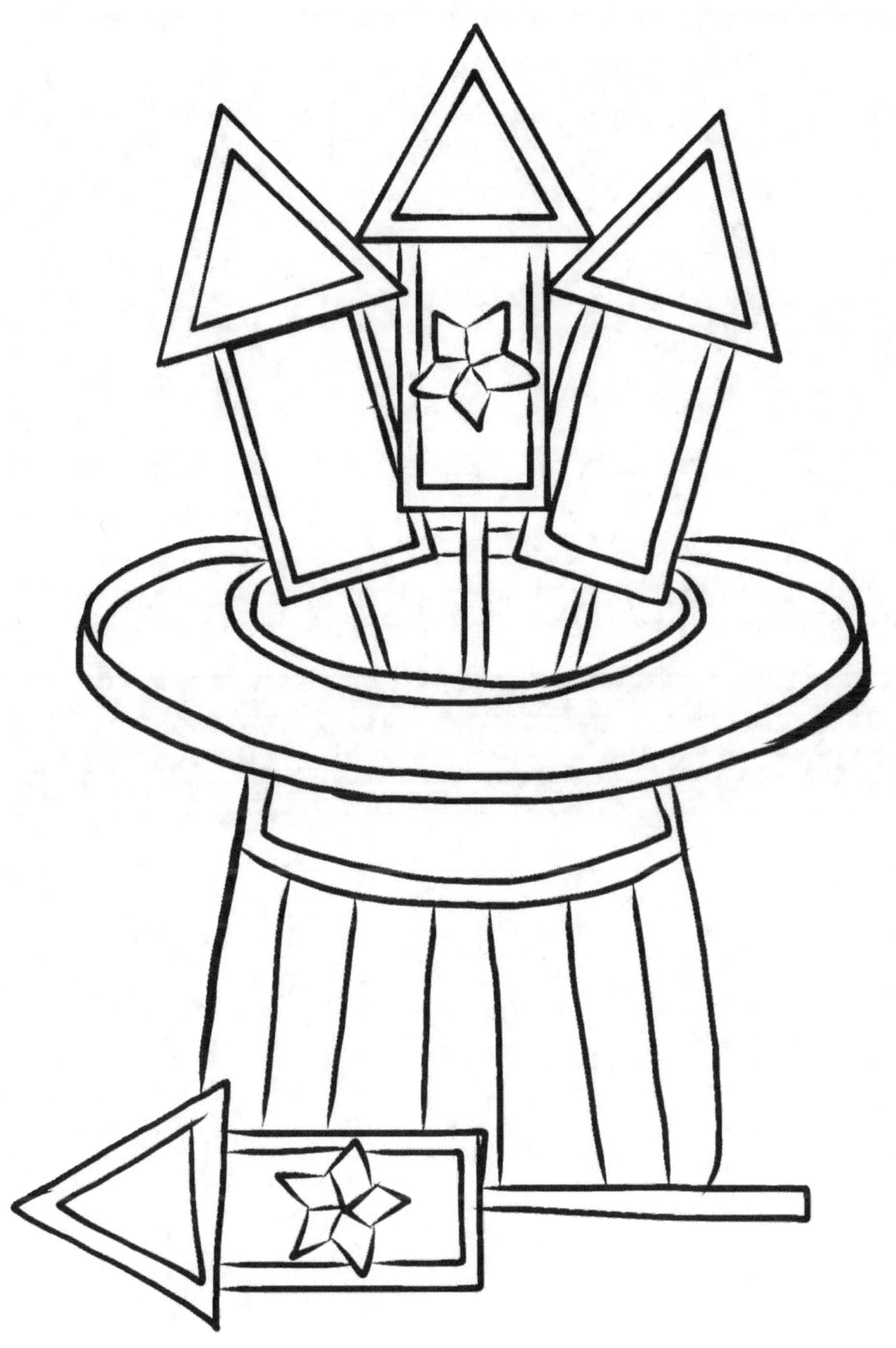

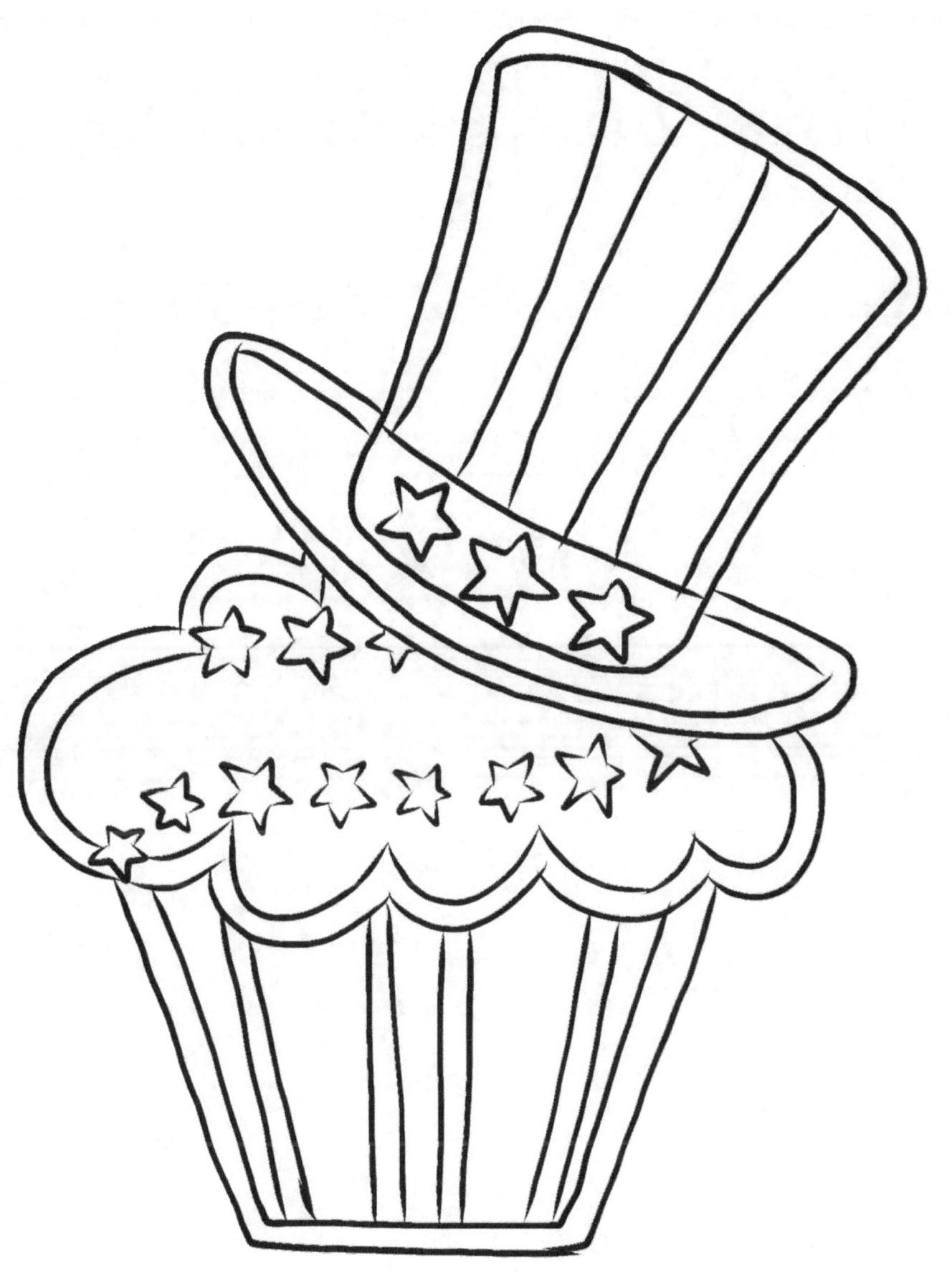

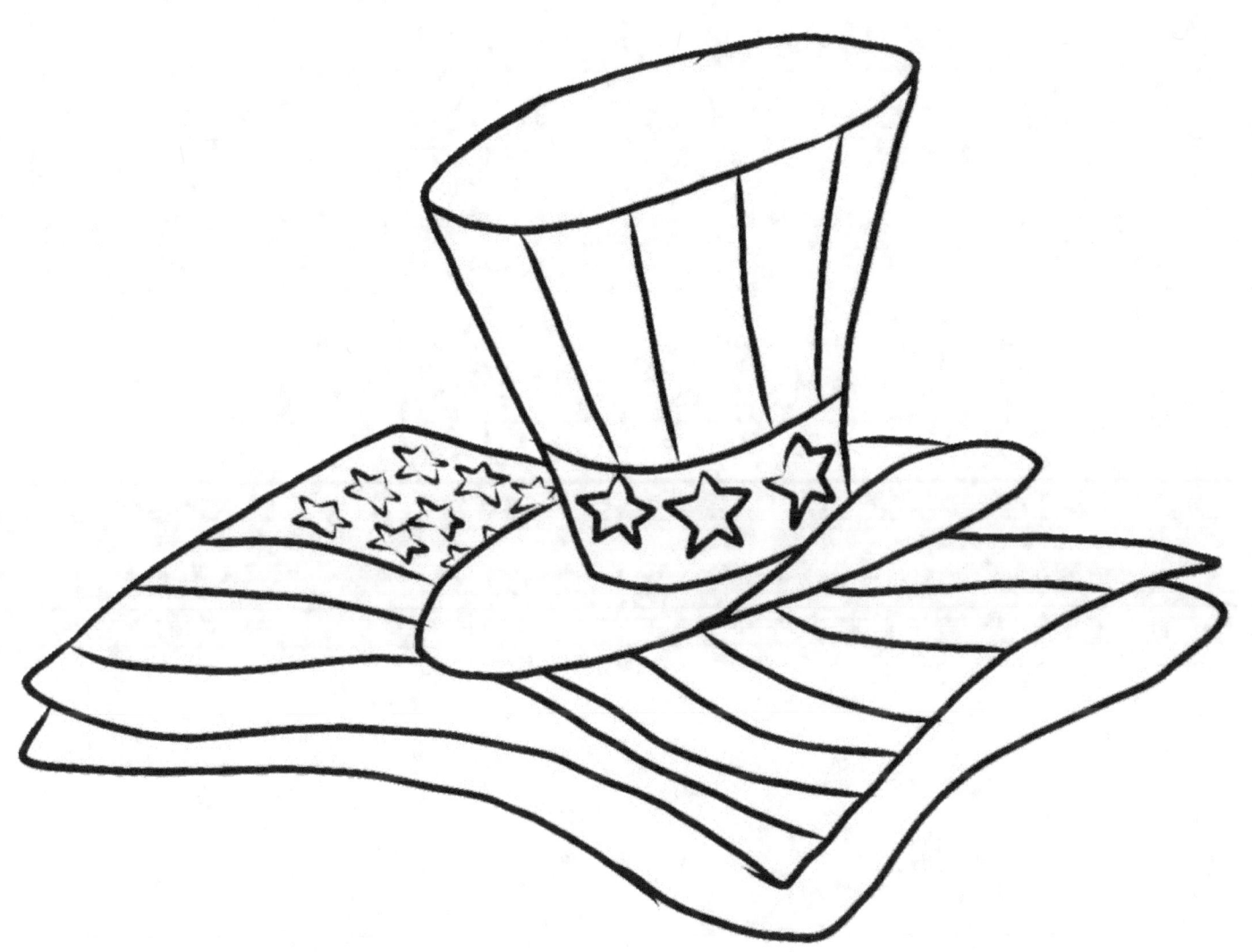

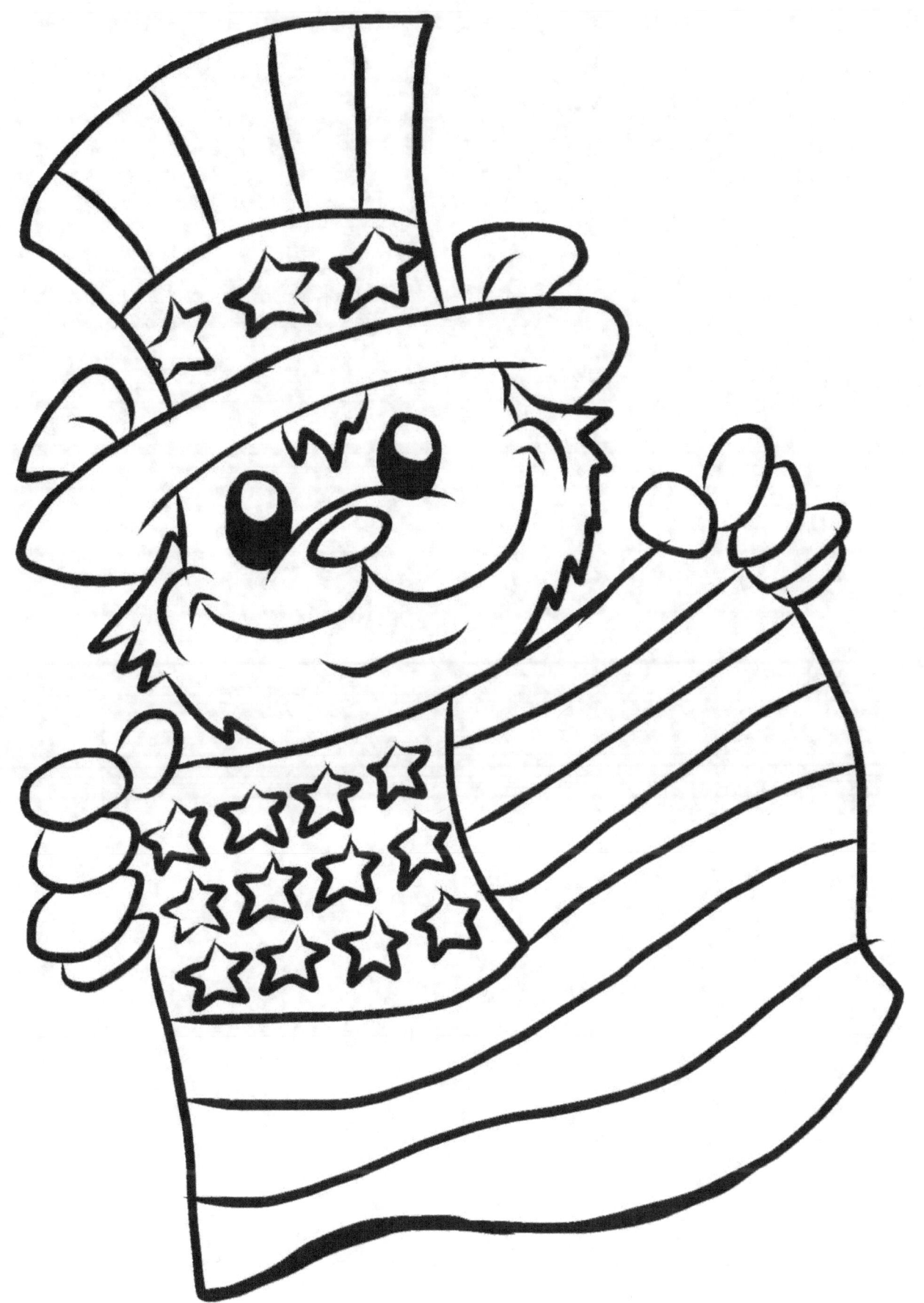

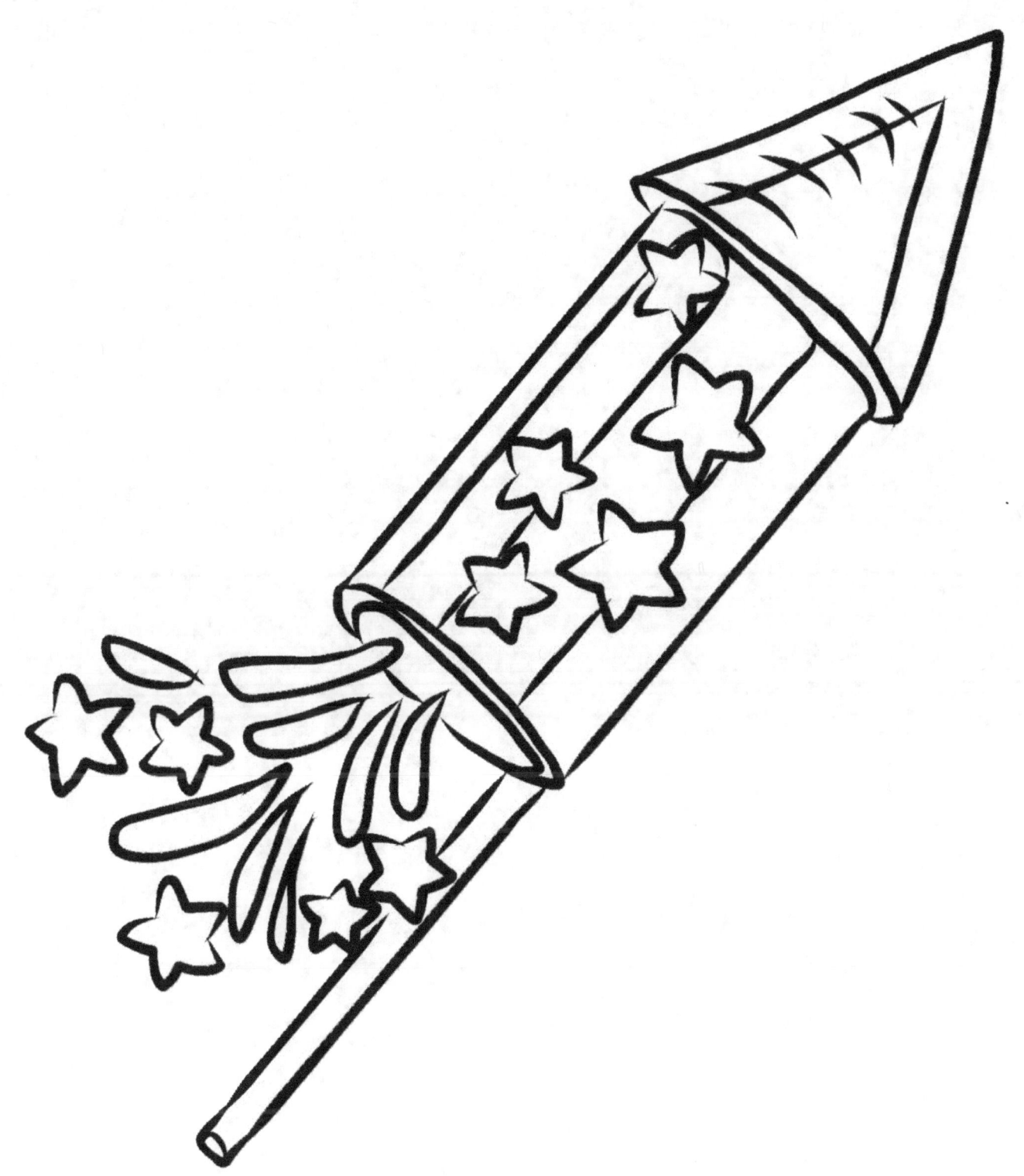

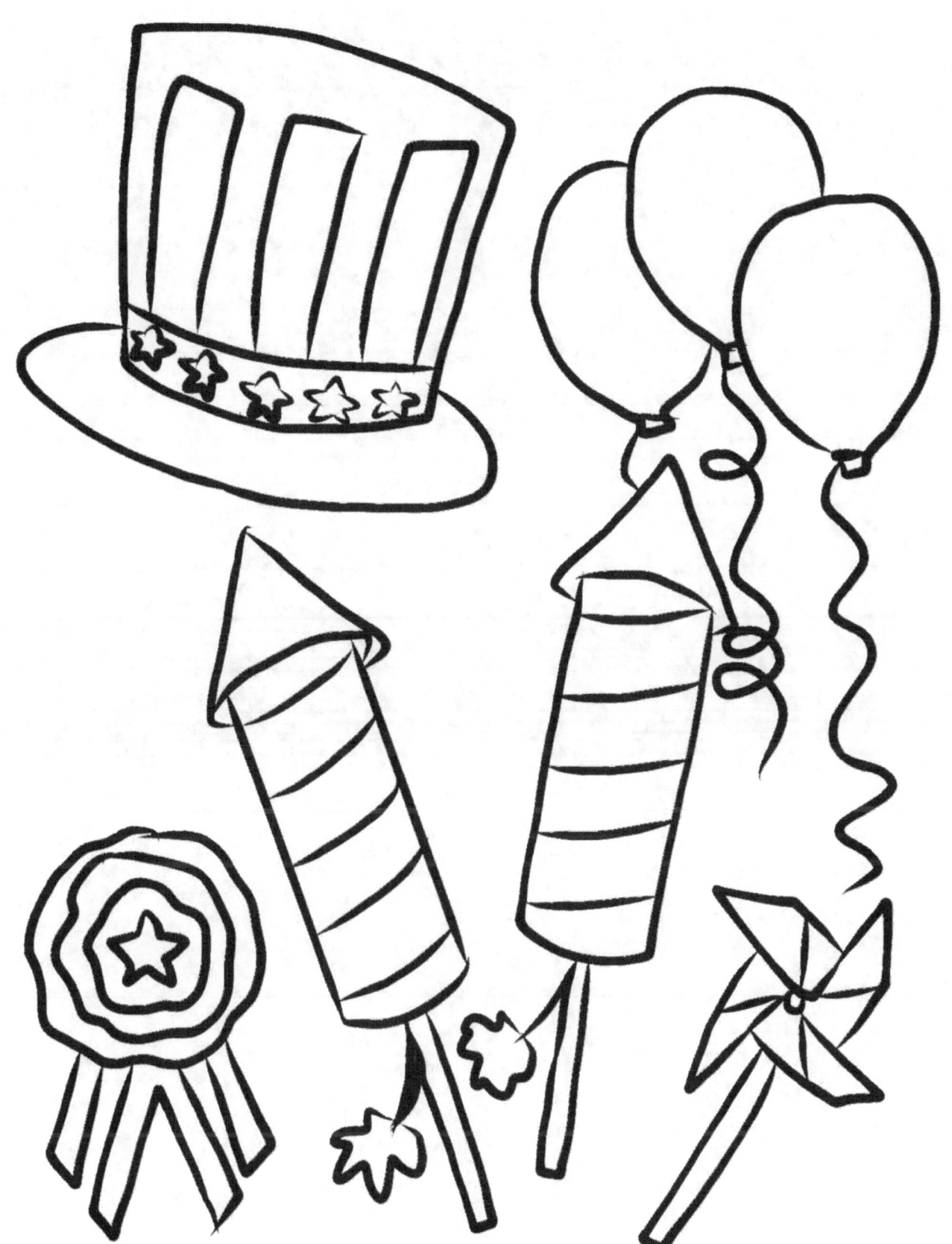

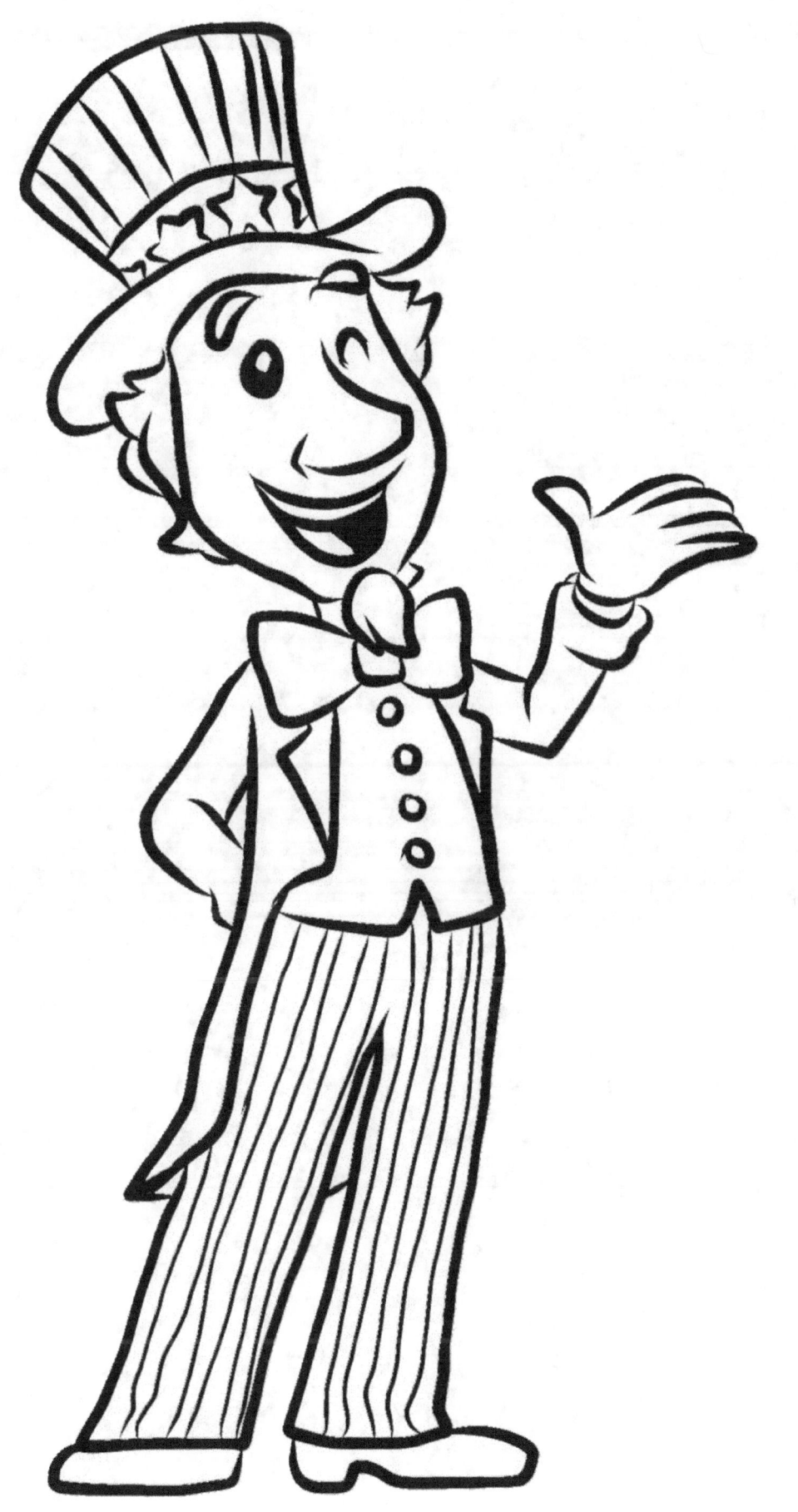

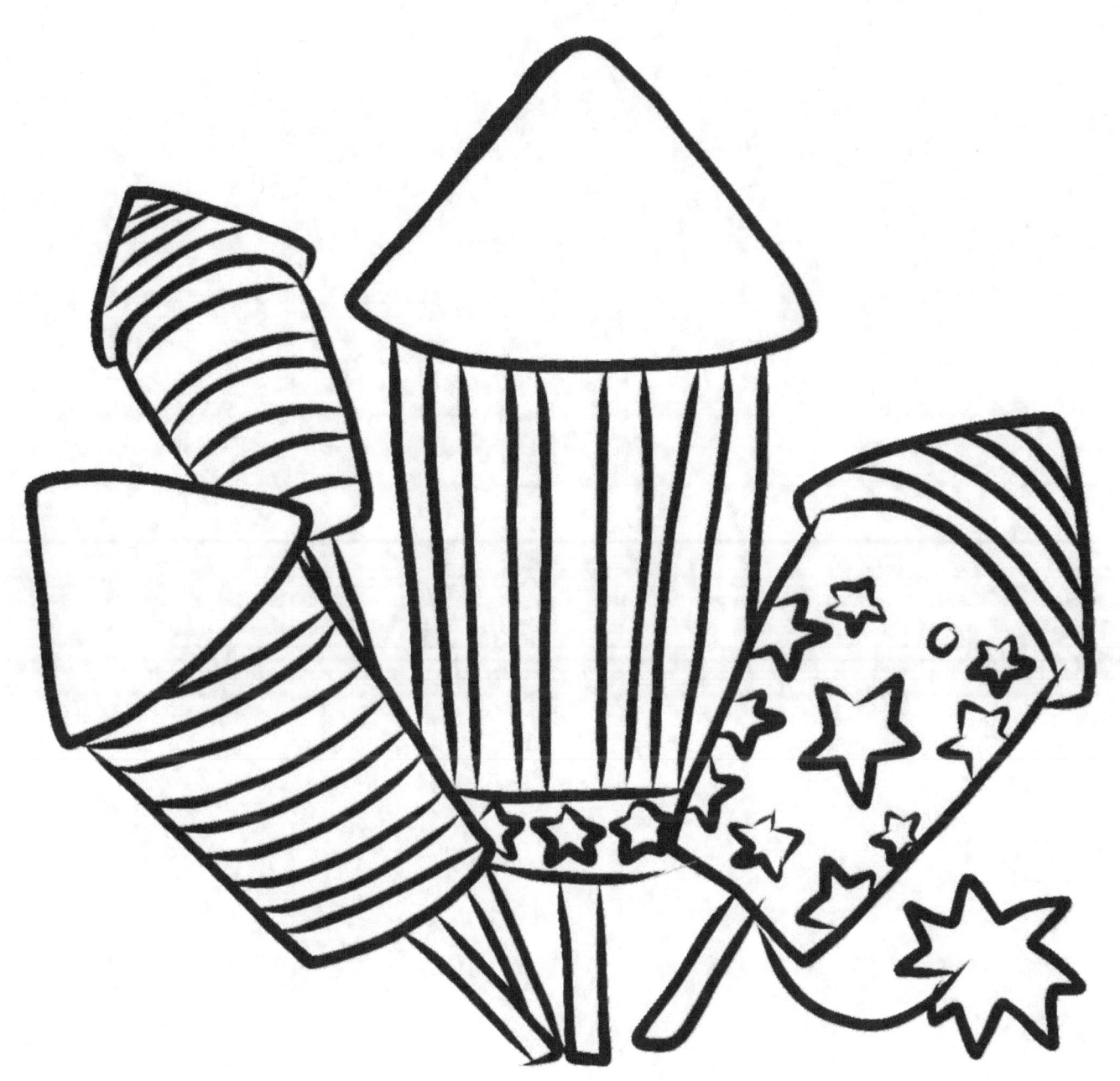

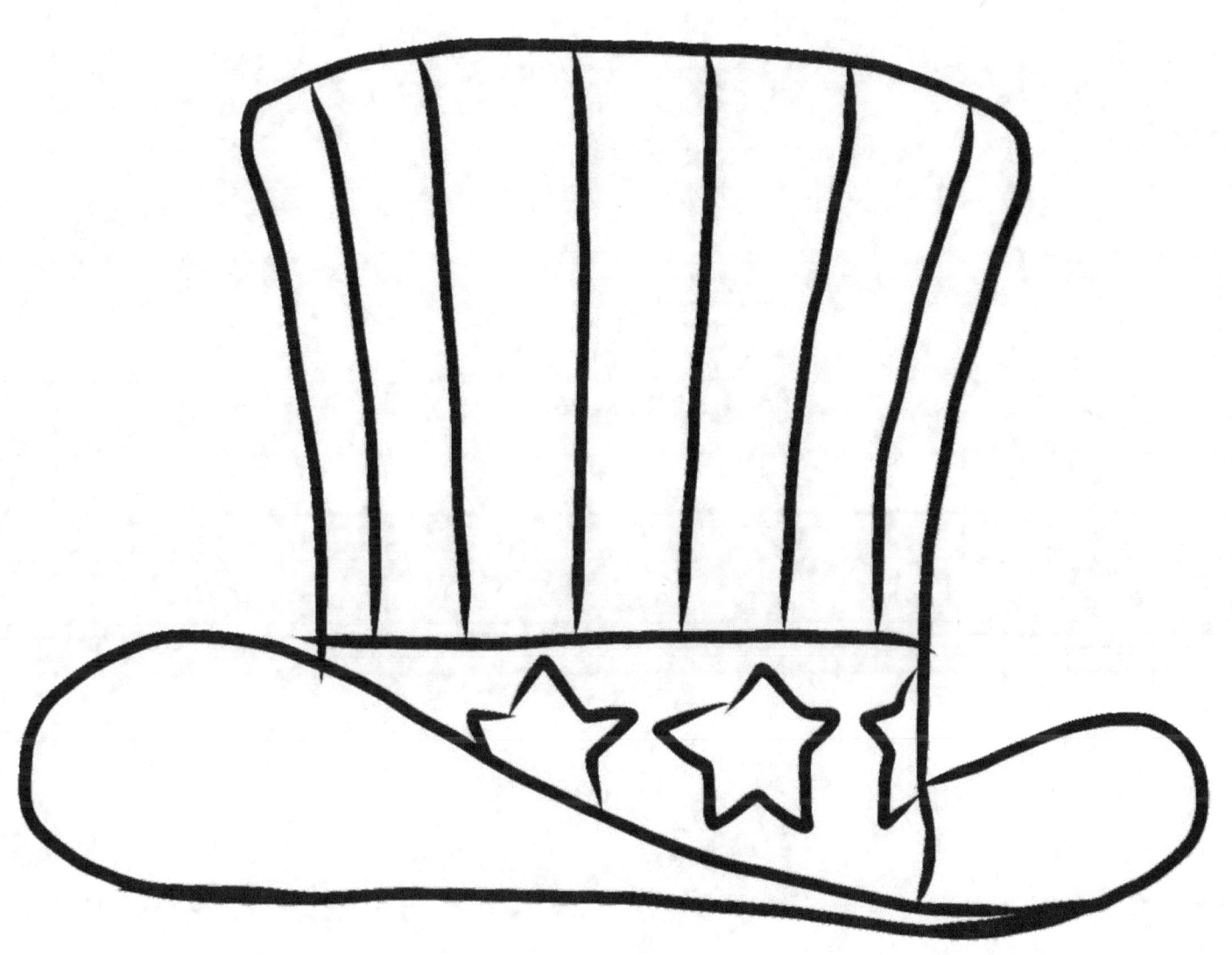

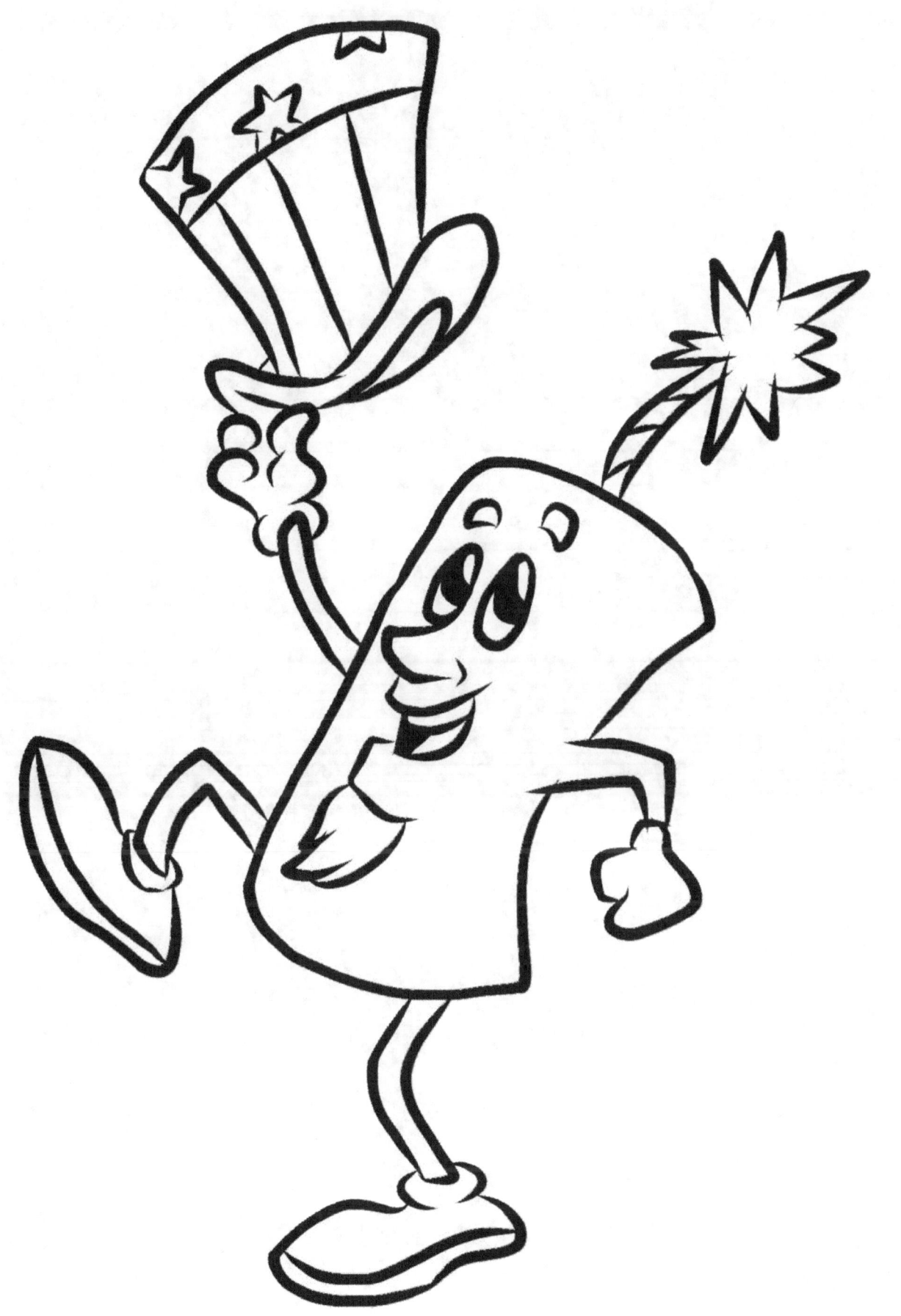

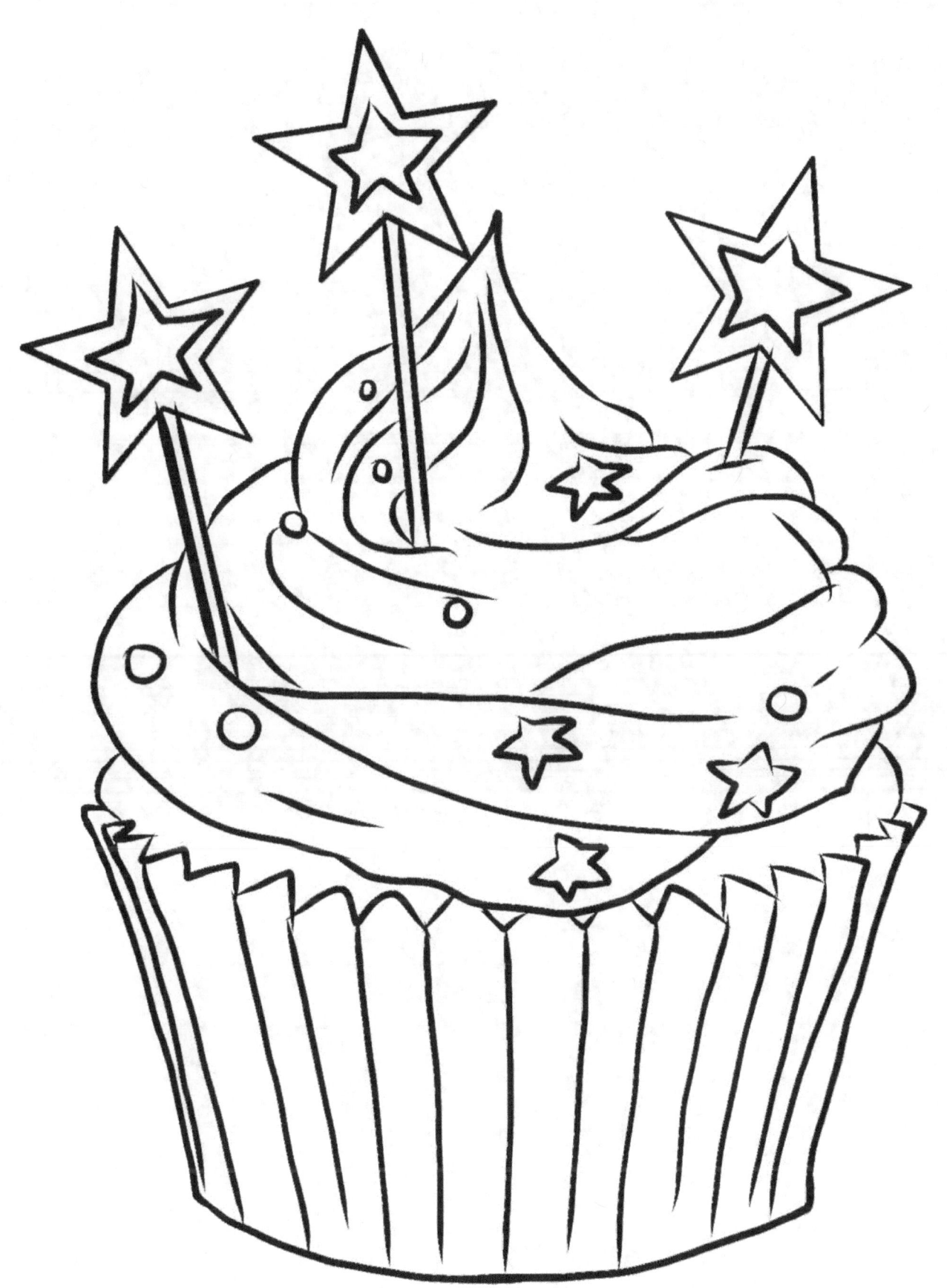

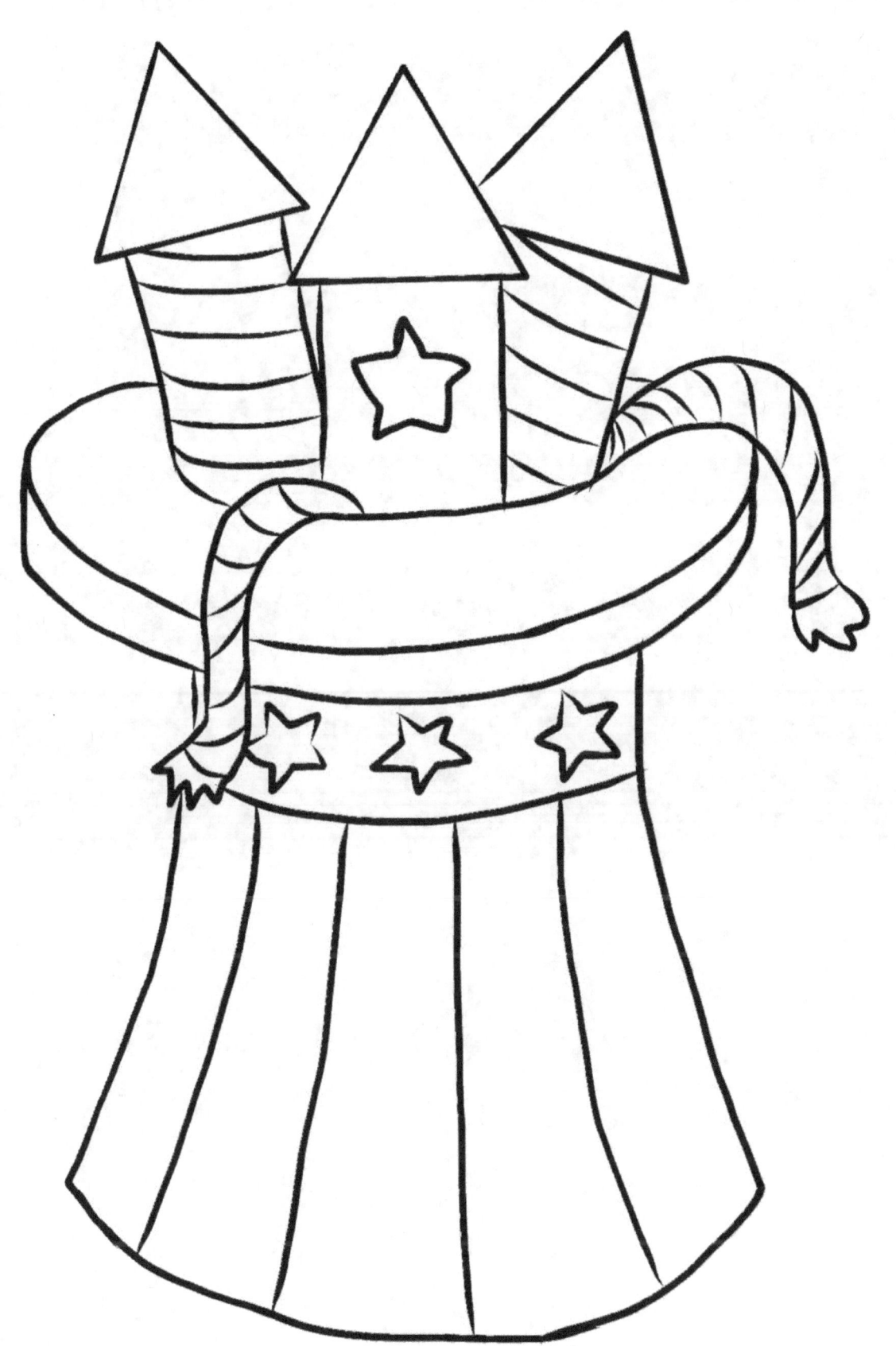

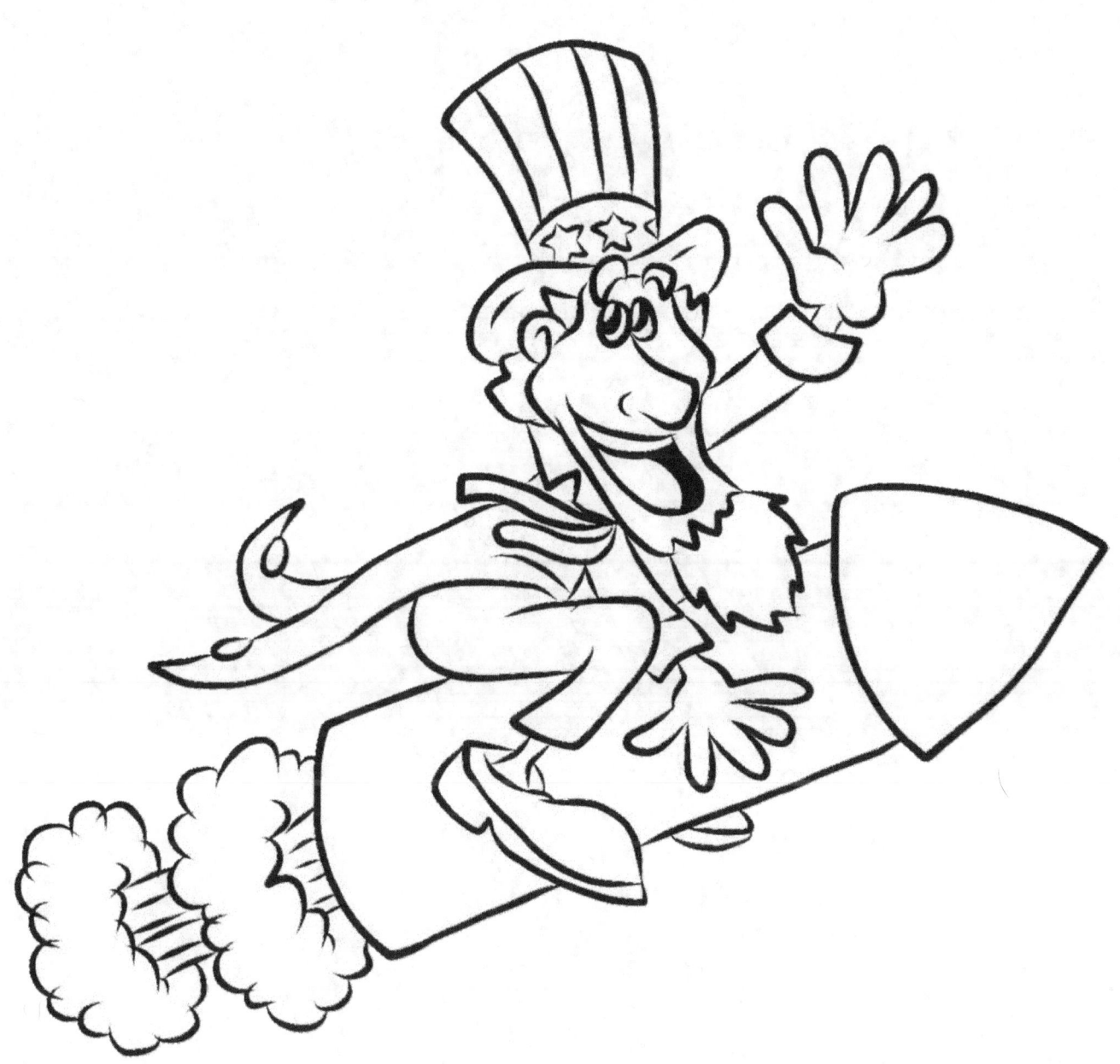

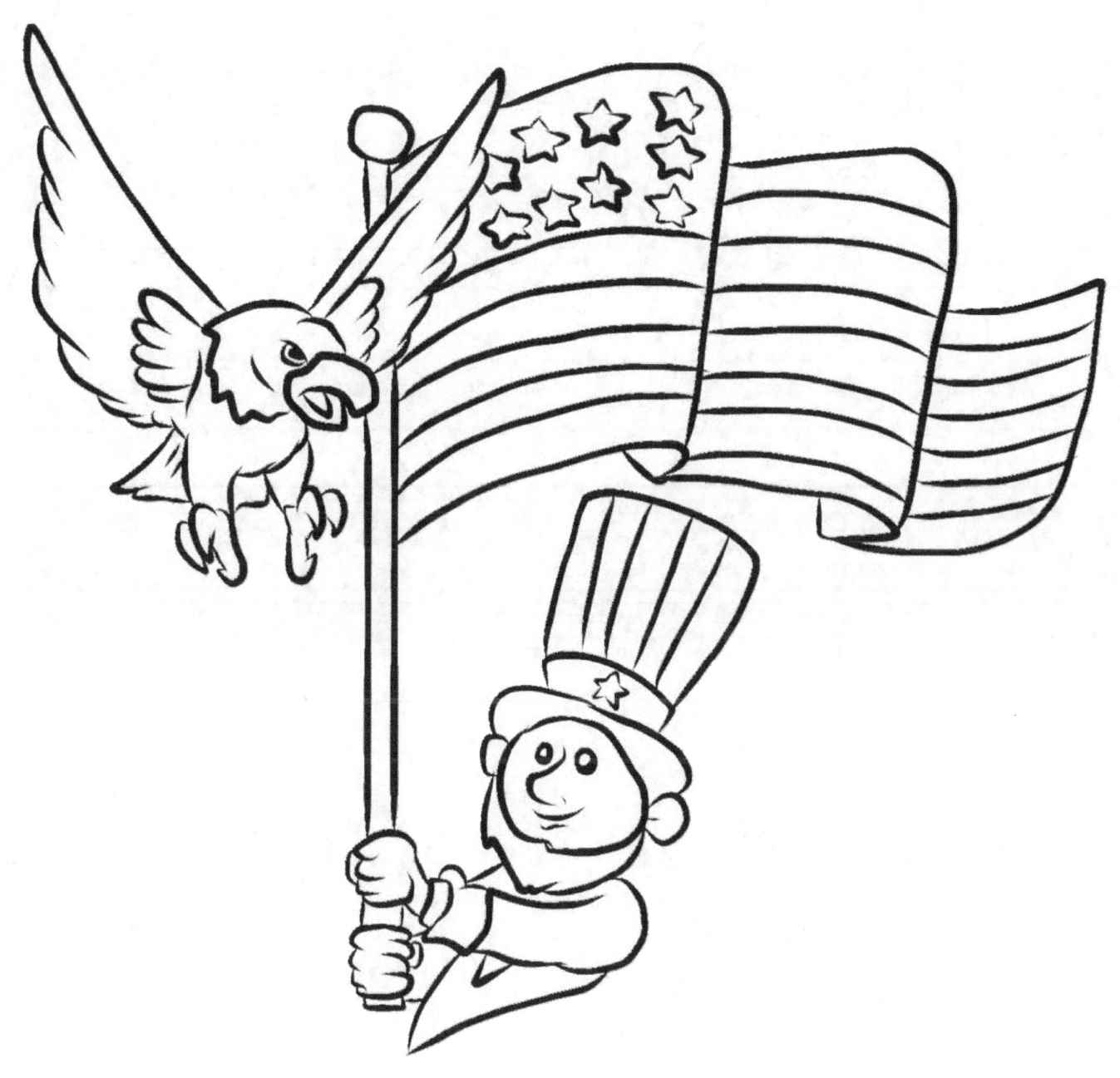

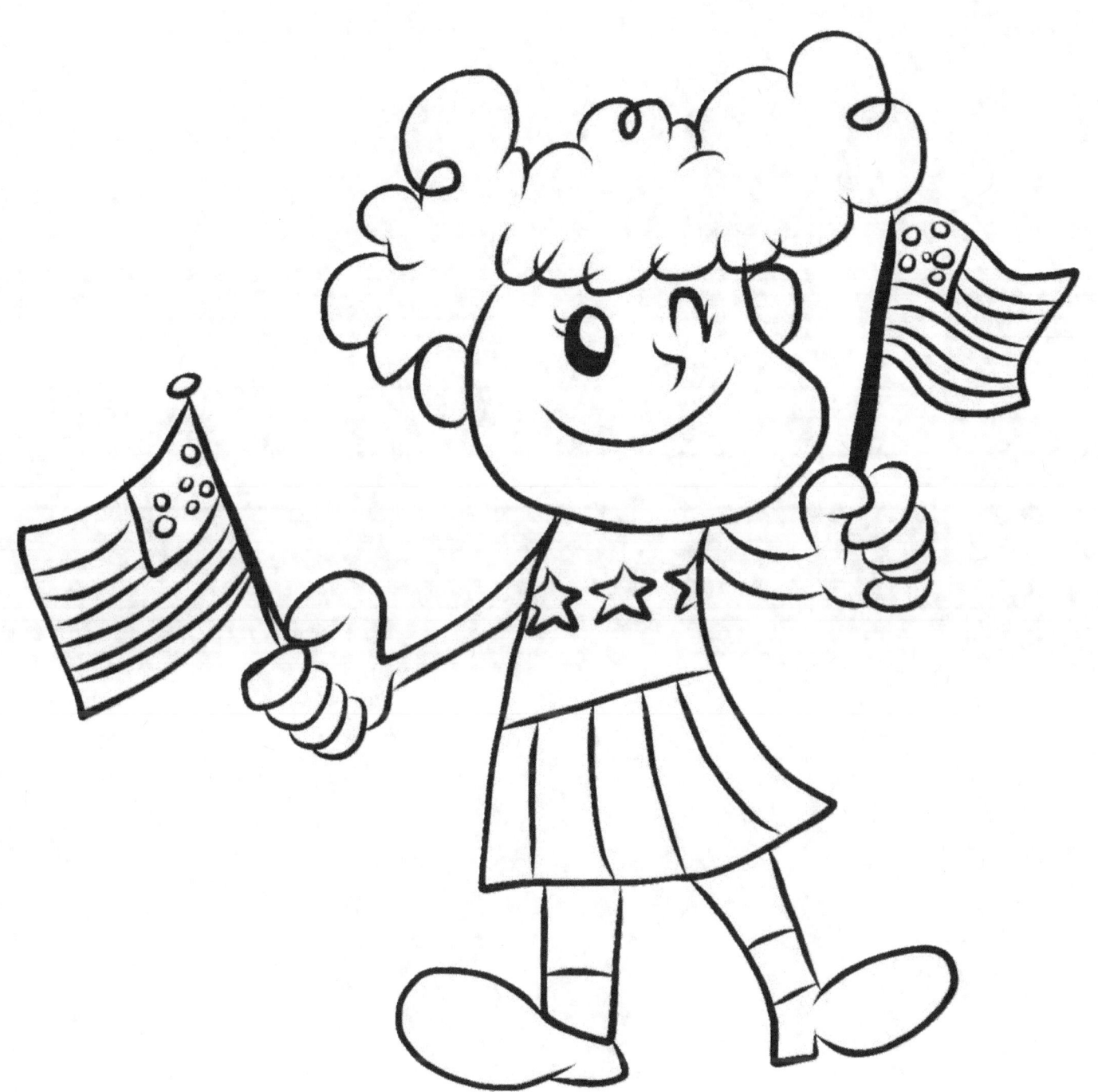

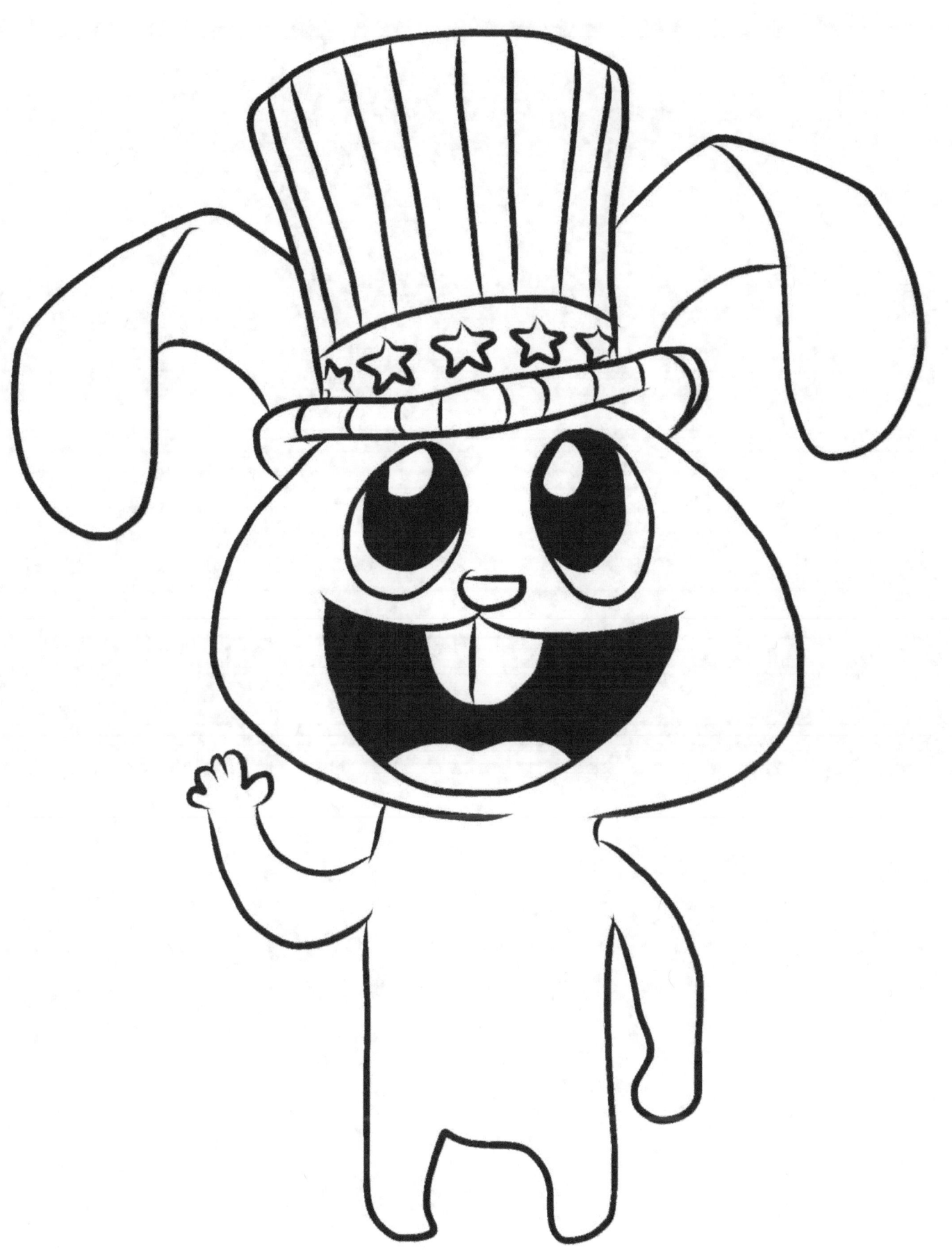

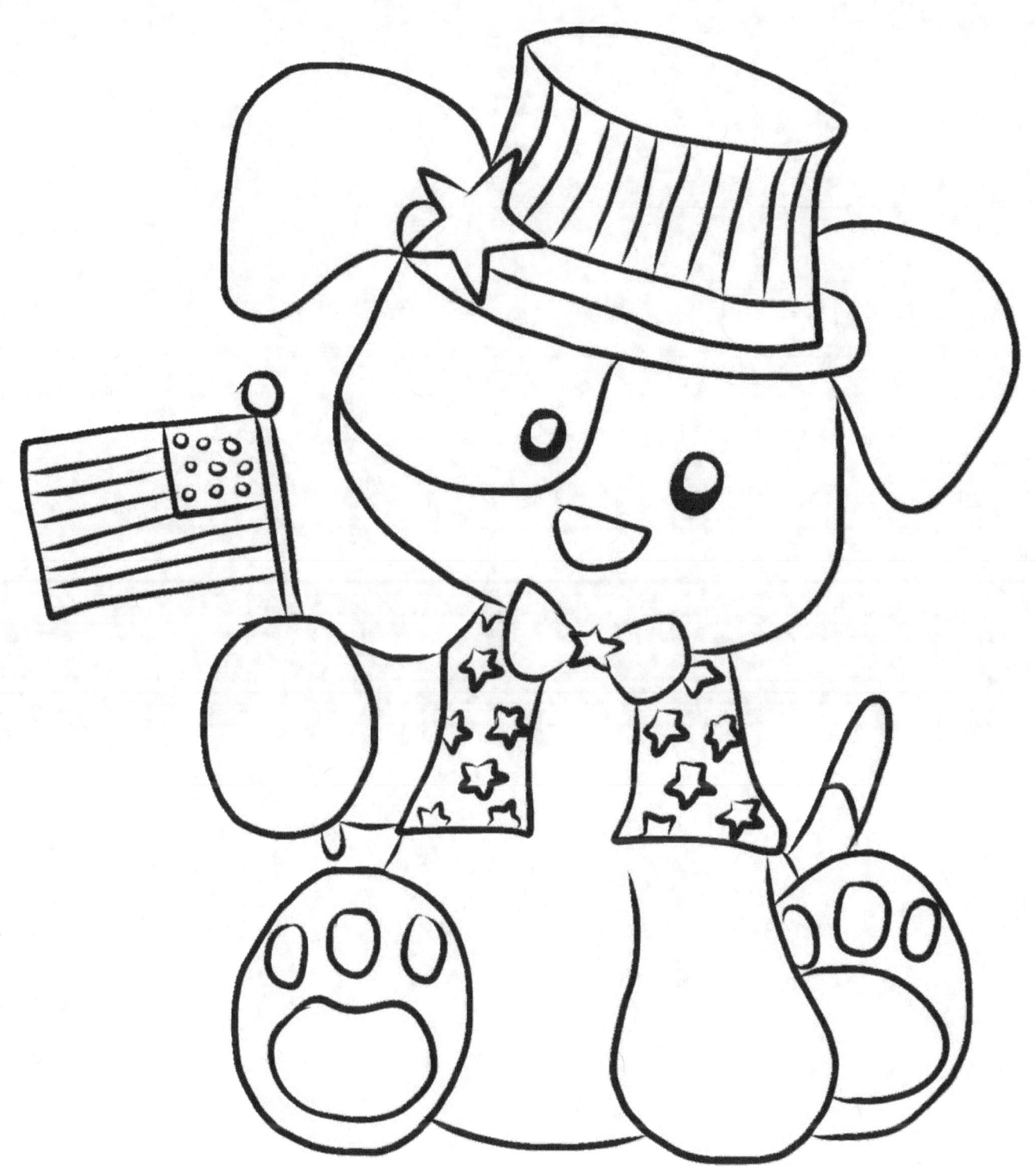

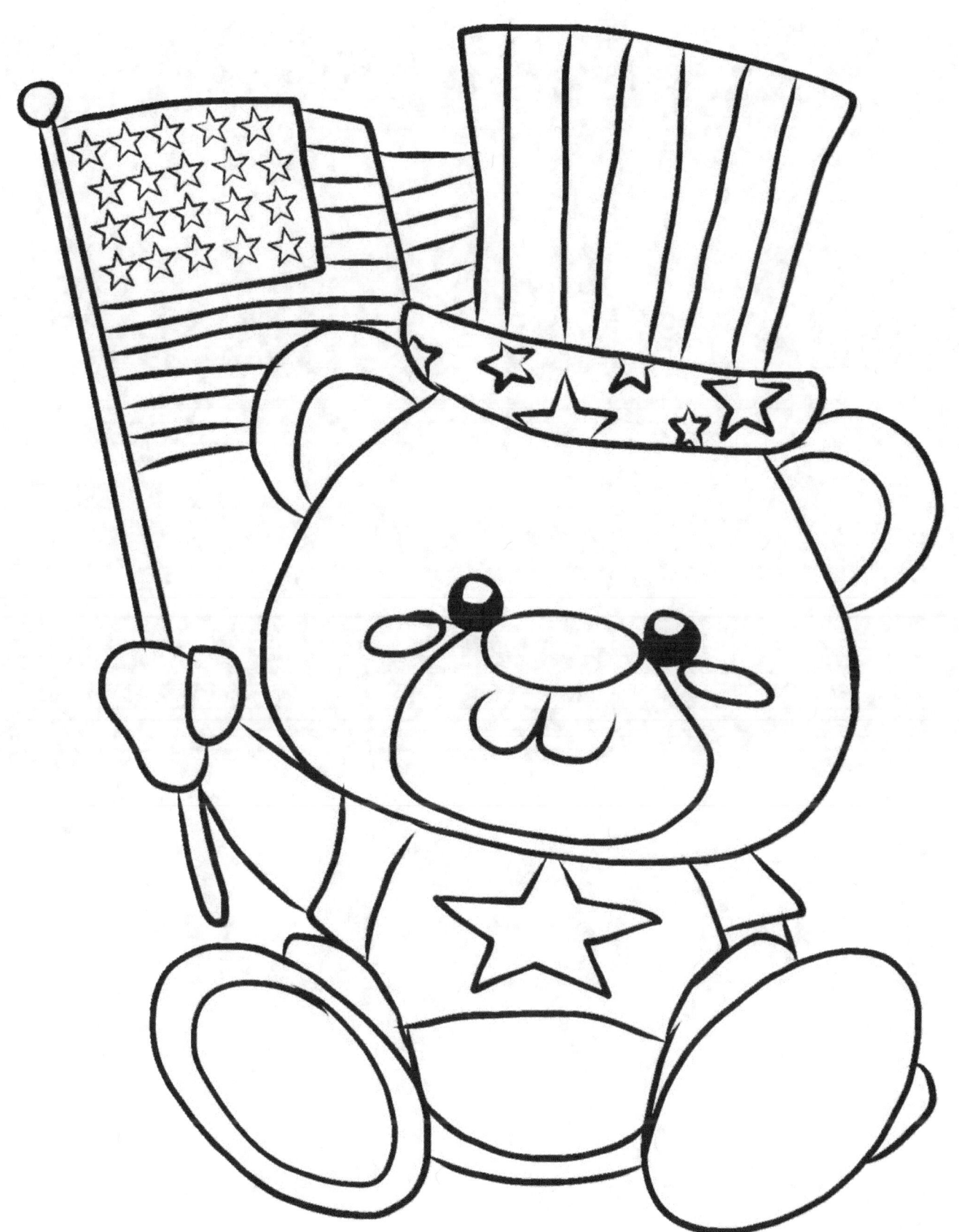

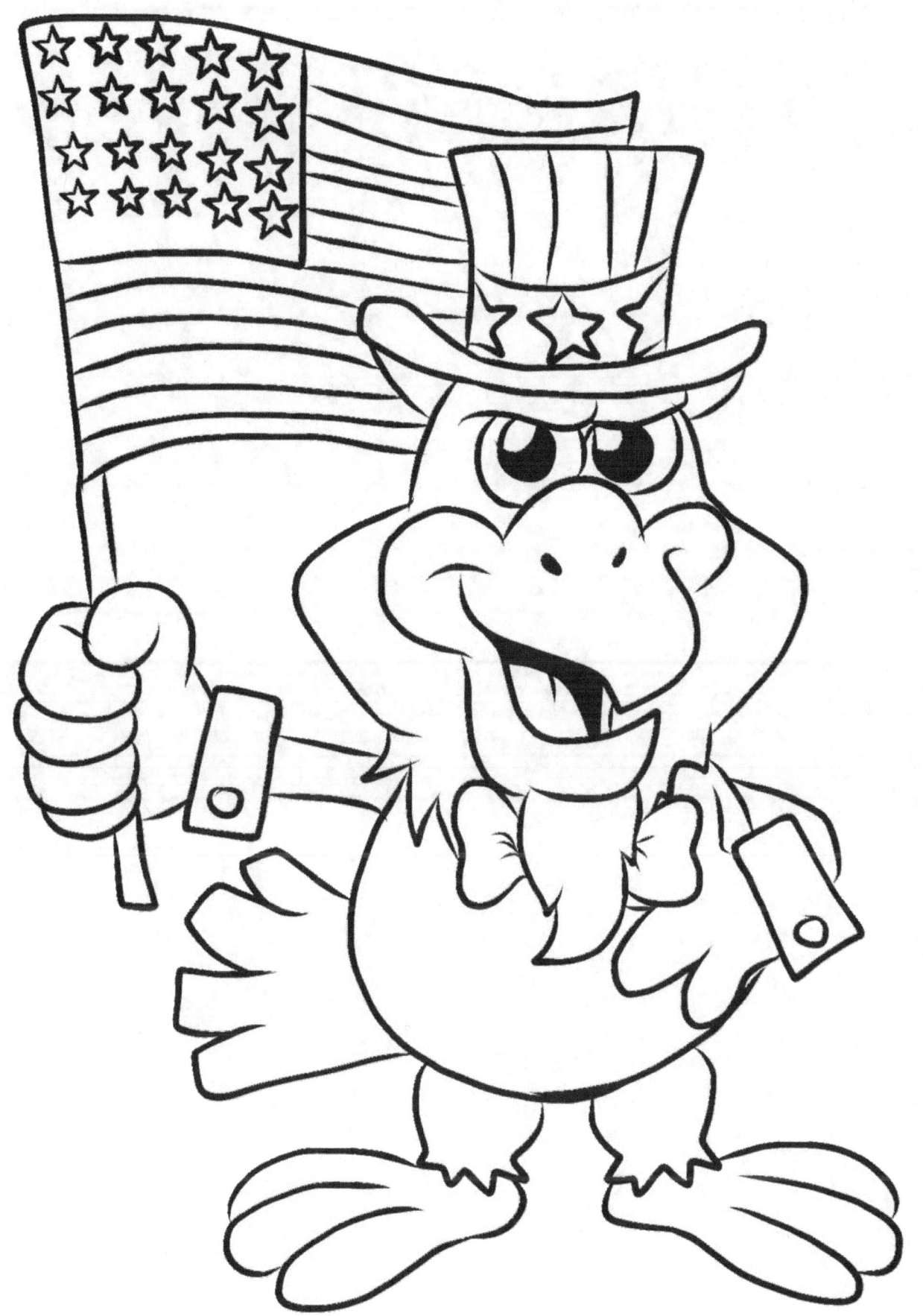

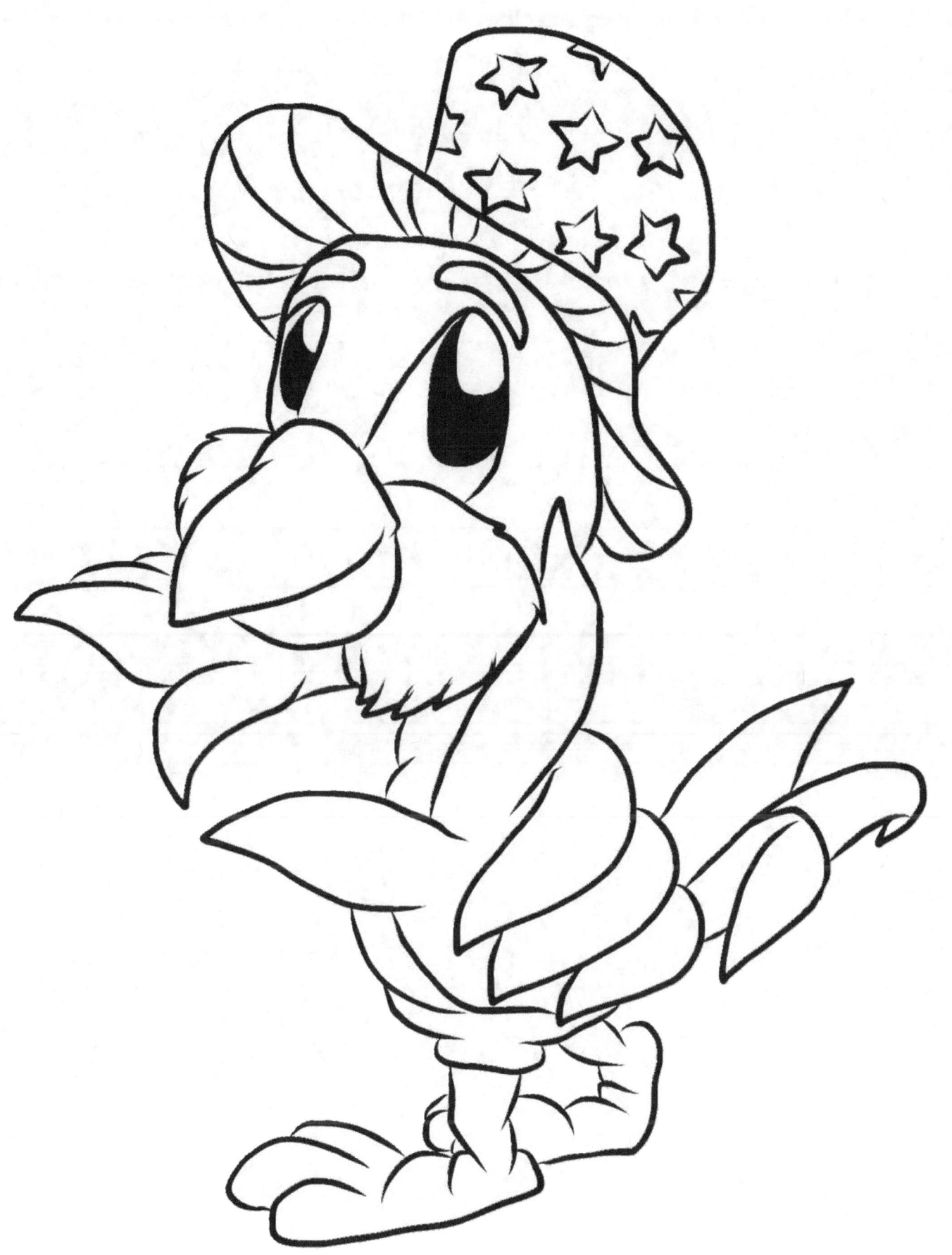

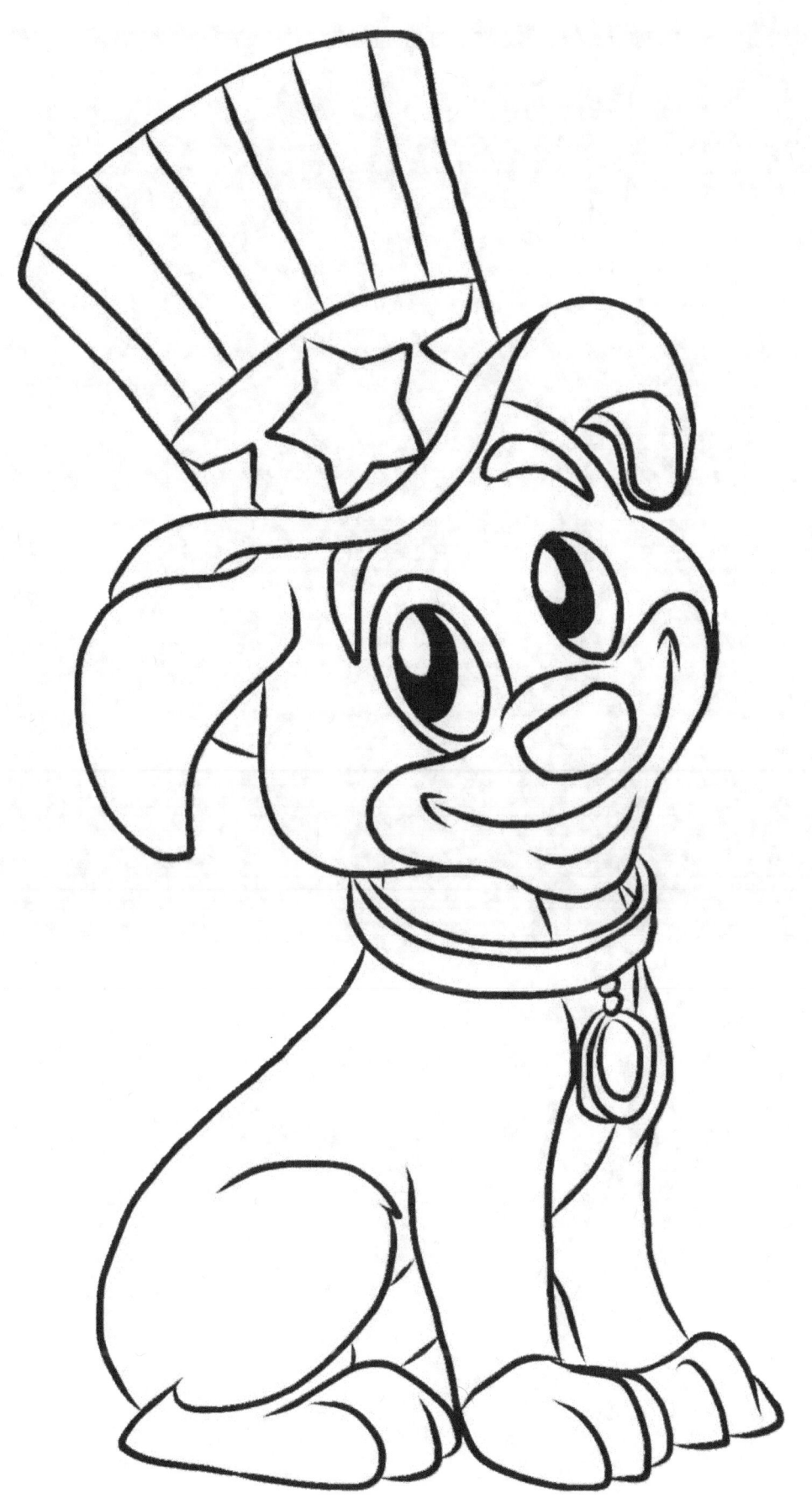

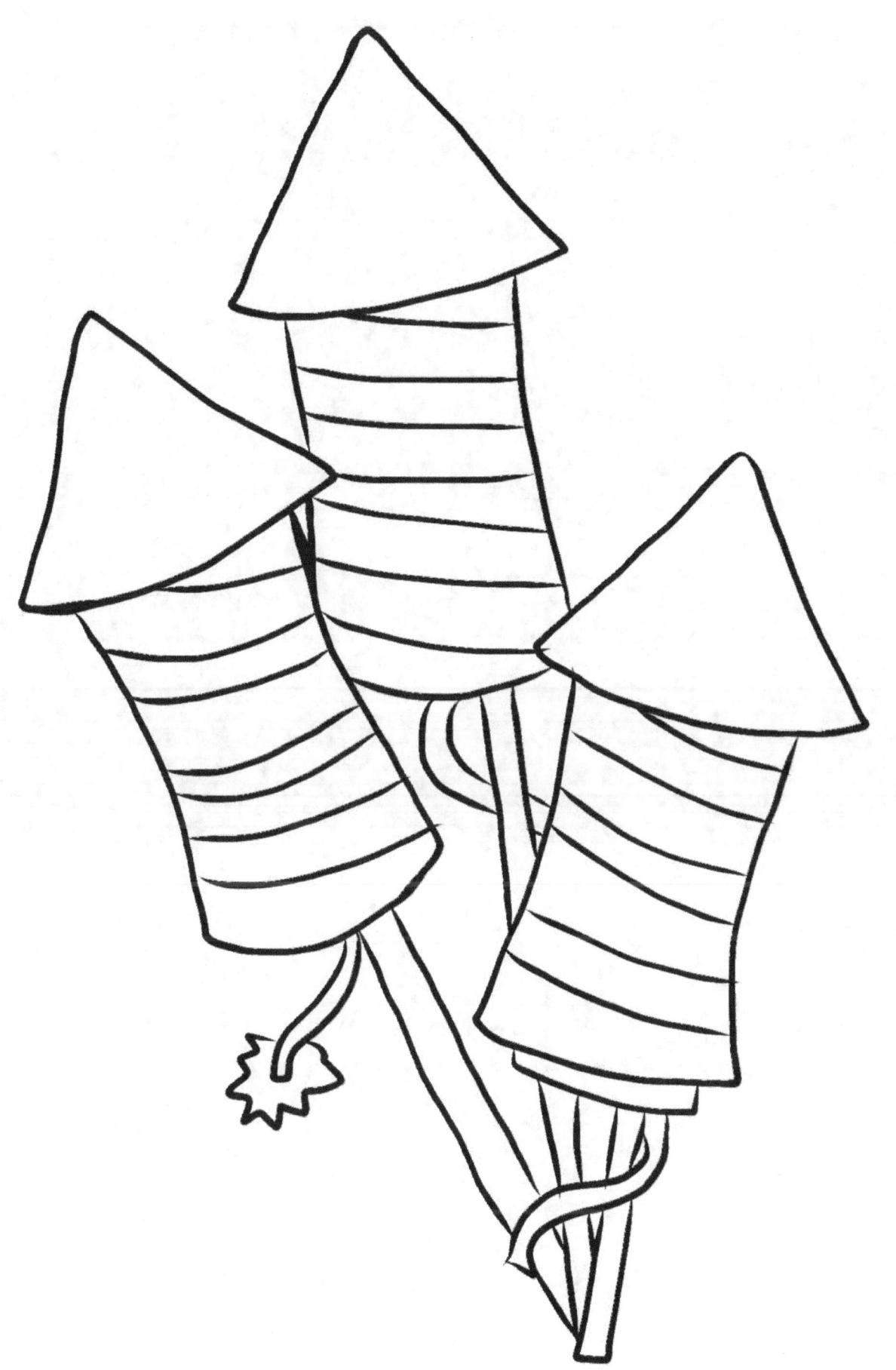

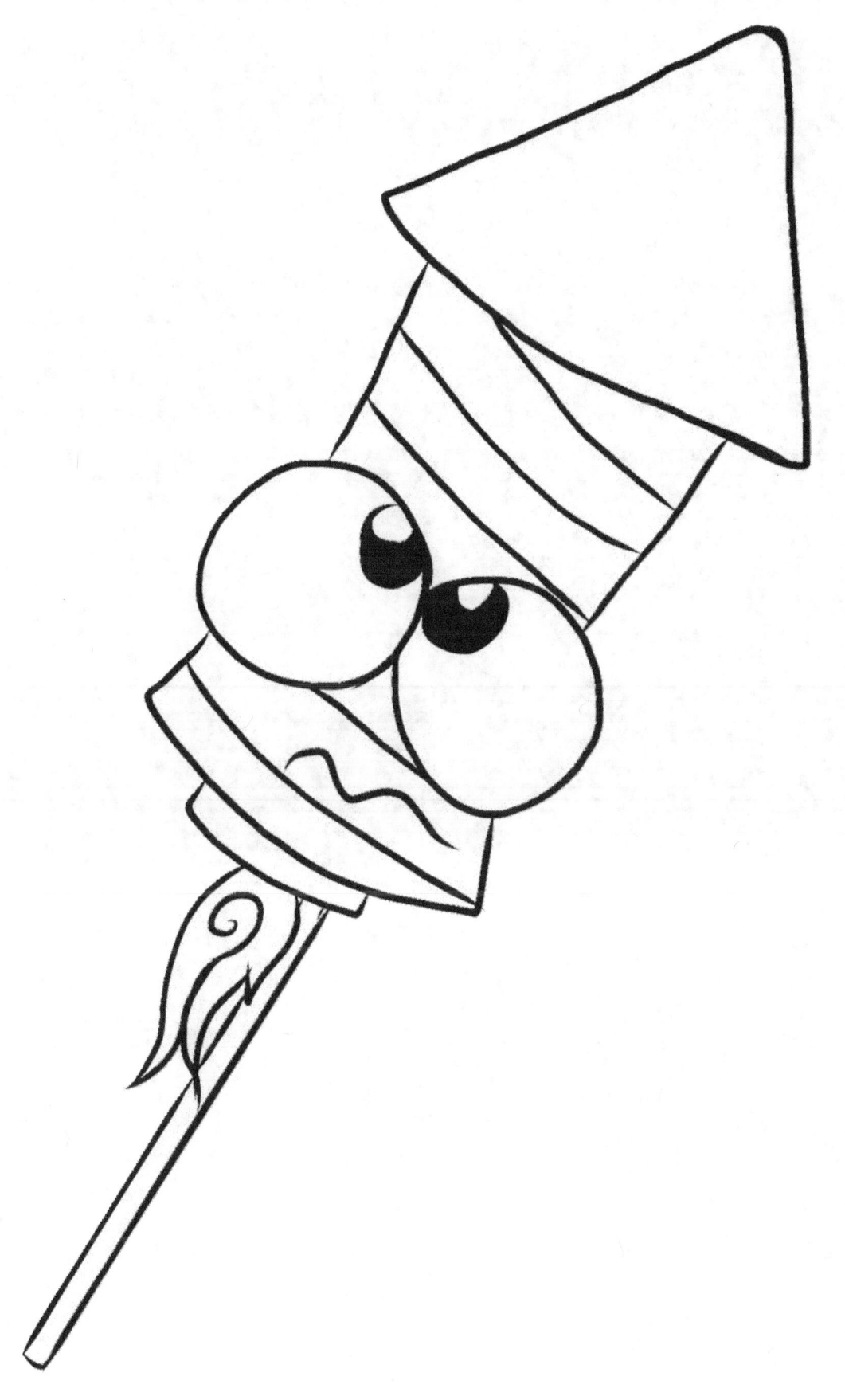

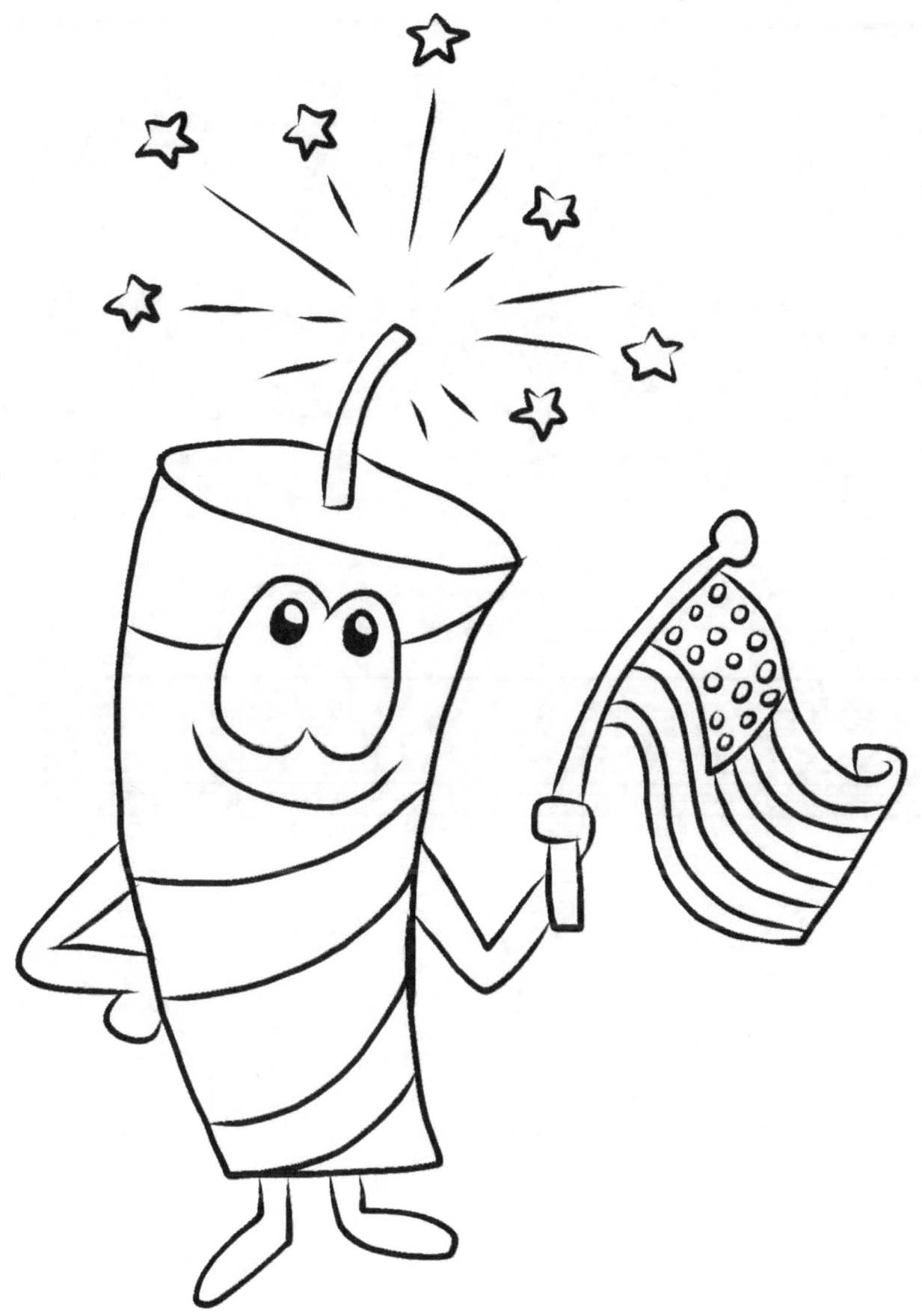

www.ingramcontent.com/pod-product-compliance
Lightning Source LLC
Chambersburg PA
CBHW060004230526
45472CB00008B/1942